FATHER COURAGE

FATHER
COURAGE

*What Happens When
Men Put Family First*

SUZANNE BRAUN LEVINE

HARCOURT, INC.
New York   San Diego   London

Library of Congress Cataloging-in-Publication Data
Levine, Suzanne.
Father courage: what happens when men put family first/Suzanne Braun Levine.
p.   cm.
Includes bibliographical references.
ISBN 0-15-100382-3
1. Fathers—United States. 2. Parenting—United States. 3. Family—United States.
4. Work and family—United States. 5. Sex role—United States.
6. Sexual division of labor—United States. I. Title.
HQ759 .L475 2000
306.874'2—dc21   99-053156

Designed by G. B. D. Smith
Text set in New Caledonia
Printed in the United States of America
First edition
A B C D E F G H I J

For Bob

CONTENTS

CONTENTS

ACKNOWLEDGMENTS

MY GRATITUDE BEGINS with my brilliant editor Jane Isay who, with my agent Michael Carlisle, made this first book not only possible but great fun. In addition I thank the Bauman Foundation and Patricia Bauman for her encouragement, support, and revolutionary spirit, and the Media Studies Center of the Freedom Forum and my fellow 1998 Fellows for providing an ideal working and thinking environment.

With an undertaking such as this, creative networking and free-form conversations that produce insights, revisions, and choice morsels of research make all the difference. Those listed here, and others I may have overlooked, gave all that and much more: Myrna Blyth, Roz Chernoff, David Cohen, Susan Dworkin, Osborn Elliott, Amanda George, Marcia Gillespie, Carol Gilligan, Jennifer Kelly, Ethel Klein, James A. Levine, Paula Marsili, Rachel Myers, Holly Peterson, Roger Rosenblatt, Steve Rubin, Marlene Sanders, Allan

Shedlin, Alan and Gloria Siegel, Bruce Tulgan and Debby Applegate, and June Zeitlin. Most of all, I am grateful to my mother, Esther Braun, who sets an inspiring example of perseverance; my Wymmin friends, who know about laughter; and my darling children, Joshua and Joanna, who are daily reminders of what really matters.

PREFACE

MY FIRST CLUE was the backpacks. Ever since my own husband began walking our children to school, I had become aware of the small band of men in my neighborhood who did the same. I enjoyed witnessing those rare occasions of public fathering, when a man was on his own as a parent. So when the pattern began to change, I became curious. Not only were there more of them than in the past, but something about them said the newcomers were not once-a-season show-off dads, but the real thing. The "something" was the profusion of pink and yellow and red cartoon-character backpacks slung over their shoulders. Like the moms and baby-sitters trudging by, they seemed blissfully oblivious to giant rabbit or Mickey Mouse ears rising from behind their own. Only a parenting pro knows how relieving the little student of his or her baggage releases a certain delicious bounce and chatter. These were dads who *knew*—knew their own kids in that everyday way.

I began to ask questions, not only of the fathers in my neighborhood, but of those who watch out for major social trends. The more I talked to people, the more convinced I became that the Mickey Mouse ears were the tip of the iceberg, so to speak.

Now, it isn't all that hard to go a block or two out of the way to escort your children to school on the way to work—especially if you have left the breakfast dishes in the sink and someone else got up early to pack the lunch and stayed up late blow-drying the clay volcano being so proudly borne on a cardboard tray. Lots of men do that, and sometimes they get more credit than their wives think they deserve for inconveniencing themselves even that much. But the ones I had begun to notice and hear about were standing out because they seemed to be really investing themselves in their children's lives. That commitment, whether they are aware of it or not, poses a challenge to the traditional separation of church (home) and state (paid work), the separation of the world of women and the world of men.

That challenge, coming from the male side, forms a yin–yang with the efforts of women to break out of the domestic ghetto. If men are able to break free of the expectations imposed on them because they are men and integrate themselves into the fabric of family life, they will make the circle whole—and, like the women of the seventies, enlarge their own experience in ways they can only imagine. They will also help make the fullness of human experience more accessible to their sons and daughters.

I wondered what the second half of the revolution would be like. Would men, who have so much going for them in the status quo, be willing to make the same kind of effort their mothers and sisters had made to change the rules? Were they ready to do the dirty work? Make the trade-offs?

So far the men I've talked to don't feel part of any larger effort; if anything, they feel out of step, they told me. Among the chatting women at the school door, they are odd men out, and at work, they are letting down the team if they allow their "other life" to intrude.

As a result, most are stressed-out and fearful of slipping up. Some are resentful about how few choices they can see for themselves and how little support they get, compared to the women they work with, for their efforts to blend work and family. Others are angry about not being appreciated at home, but afraid of admitting it, because they know there is so much more they could be doing. But as they talked about such things—many, I am sure, for the first time—one beat got louder and louder. It was an anthem that each played in his own heart: As these men told me over and over again, they were trying to become the fathers they wish they had.

The fathers we all wish we had. We all have dream dads, characters in books or on television or other people's fathers who looked pretty good to a kid, but we have little firsthand experience to draw on when reality strikes. My own father, a busy surgeon, adored me and my brother in his way, but I would no sooner have looked to him for silliness or under-standing than I would for dinner. The only day-to-day con-tact we had was when he drove me to school every morning. I can still hear us chanting as the building came into view, "I see, I see, icy, icy...."

My husband is much more there for our children, who are now teenagers, than his own father, who was warm but bewildered by the role. His involvement is not enough for me, both for my own peace of mind and what I perceive would be the richness in their lives. But I can't speak from any more experience than he can about what that good dad would be like.

THE SEARCH FOR GOOD DADS

My random conversations led to more serious research, lots of reading and dozens of long interviews with fathers who had been referred to me because they seemed to be walking the walk as well as talking the talk. The books helped me un-derstand what expectations have been imposed on men growing up in the last half of the twentieth century. The news coverage, which was almost nonexistent, helped me sense how invisible the men I wanted to understand must feel. But it was the fathers themselves who brought their struggle into focus for me. As they explained what they were attempting to do, I came to respect their determination, even as I saw over and over again how they were falling short.

I could imagine, though, that it was the one step back rather than the two steps forward that got more attention from their wives. I know the wives very well—I've experienced their exhaustion, impatience, ambivalence; their resentment at their husbands' freedom to choose when and where to be an "involved parent." The skepticism most women, myself included, feel about equal male parents is conveyed in the recurrent "rolling eyes" expression I get whenever the subject comes up. Nevertheless, I decided against going after both sides of every family story. I wanted the men I interviewed to feel safe from contradiction and second-guessing. I felt I could count on my years of journalism—and years of marriage—for the skepticism required to keep their claims in perspective. Even so, the more I listened, the more I was touched by the efforts of so many men to "get it" as a parent and to create a balance in their lives between work, marriage, and children.

I had been prepared to uncover a litany of workplace put-downs and disincentives, and I did: the double message that even the most "family-friendly" organizations project, the unabated pressure on a man to perform at work as if he had no other life, the lack of flexibility in hours and patterns of work, the lack of sufficient governmental support for families, and the major professional and financial sacrifices parents are forced to make.

What I was less prepared to find was a similar litany of barriers and obstacles at home. The closer I looked, the more I saw and the more this book became about marriage as well as fatherhood. My focus expanded from wanting to tell about the small but growing number of men who are trying to change the rules of family life to exploring the dynamics of family life that make it even harder to do. Why were men and women of goodwill with the best intentions having such a hard time working together?

As I got down to specifics—laundry, grocery lists, no-show baby-sitters, strep throat, and tantrums—I came up against the complications caused by assumptions that are at cross-purposes. For example, if every time a couple deals with a problem, his objective is to find a solution and hers is to learn from the process, neither will feel understood; if he has trouble shifting gears from one task to another while she lives in a frenzy of multitasking, they will not be able to share housework simply by devoting an equal number of hours a week to it; if she wants to talk things out and his response to conflict is to tune out, her emotional vocabulary will overwhelm him.

I found myself revisiting the notion of the enormous difference between "helping" and "sharing." By definition, the "helper" can count on the one he is helping to break the tasks into manageable units, to give him pointers—in essence, to help him. The "sharer" is on his own. How ready, willing, and able are frazzled fathers to learn—and do without being asked—all the minute ministrations of family life that most men have not been taught? And, by the same token, how willing are women like me to relinquish the mystical powers attributed to motherhood and really share the glory as well as the housework?

Finally, I began to wonder, if men and women had the room to explore the experience of parenthood in alternative ways, which of the differences that seem immutable would vanish along with imposed limitations—and how would any differences that are real play themselves out. If parenthood were equal, how would fatherhood be different from motherhood?

The Search for Answers

Because so many of my questions had to do with marriage, all of the men whose stories I tell at length are married. That doesn't mean that there aren't single fathers who are carrying off a monumental undertaking. Seventeen percent of all single parents are men—a number that is rising every year—and I try to suggest some of the lessons we can learn from their sink-or-swim experience. But in many ways marriage is as much a part of the problem as part of the solution, so I have focused on it.

Otherwise the men you will read about are as diverse as I could make them. (I have given them pseudonyms, but the words are their own.) Everywhere I went, I met people who had friends, sons, and brothers who put family first; each one thought the one they admired was waging a solitary crusade. If nothing else, they will see in the stories that follow that such fathers are everywhere. The men I interviewed range in age from mid-twenties to early forties. Some are middle class, some quite well-off, and several are barely making ends meet. The group includes urban, suburban, and rural experiences, and although I had expected that the African Americans I spoke to would have a somewhat different story to tell, that was not the case, which is why I have not identified them by race. Many of the fathers I write about are educated; some are not, but as far as I could tell that did not affect the degree to which they were conscious of their part in a revolution. Some were and many weren't. Most of all, they felt alone and were so glad to talk.

What they wanted to talk about boiled down to one unifying commitment—each had made being part of his kids' lives a top priority. Regardless of whether he chose to do so for philosophical or political reasons or because the circumstances gave him little choice, each was making sacrifices large and small to achieve a family life. Background, cultural expectations, and even economic variations made less difference than I expected, mainly, I think, because regardless of where they come from, all men are up against what a feminist friend calls "the culture of manhood." What matters to the men in these pages, more than where they came from, is where they are going. And how unprecedented—and unrecognized—their numbers are.

The more familiar numbers are statistics about fathers who are moving out of their children's lives. Twenty-four percent of American children live in mother-only families, a dramatic increase, according to the 1997 Census. The National Fatherhood Initiative, an organization that supports "loving, committed and responsible fathers," reports that, among those fathers who are still home, working fathers spend an average of only twelve minutes per weekday one-on-one with their children—who in turn spend more time in front of the TV by age six than they will spend speaking with their fathers in their lifetime. Sadly, for all the lip service the "crisis in American families" is getting from political and religious quarters, the solutions being put forward fall short of meaningful public commitment. But a third group of fathers—those who are bucking the statistics—gets little attention or support. Increased visibility might even make them more attractive role models for all fathers.

According to the Fatherhood Initiative, data shows conclusively that "when fathers are engaged in their children's lives, their children evidence greater self-esteem, higher educational achievement, a more secure gender identity and greater success in life." The dads in this book want this for their children, but they want something for themselves, too. Educator and writer Allan Shedlin Jr. calls it the experience of "exuberant daddying." He emphasizes the rewards that come with the job. Some are ennobling: "a strong reminder of what is fundamentally important: the responsibilities and obligations of power; the importance of commitment and vulnerability; and the value of questioning, not merely finding answers." Other rewards are more "childlike," such as rekindled "curiosity, imagination, playfulness, the propensity to question, a willingness to make mistakes, a sense of wonder, enthusiasm, flexibility, and humor."

Indeed, despite the stress and anxiety and conflict they experienced, the men I interviewed all reported having fun, more fun than they had ever imagined, fun that became joy at unexpected moments. That, in the end, made their choice the only one for them. I see men in loving engagement with their children everywhere—in the hardware store, at the beach, on the bus—and I am sure that even if they aren't doing all they could, they *are* different from their fathers.

They are also part of something momentous. Several years ago I was struck by the combination of resentment and envy in a comment from a male friend. "I support the women's movement," he told me. "I just can't do anything about it." Now he can. The continuing struggle on the part of women to be taken as seriously as workers as they are as mothers has yielded many benefits for both men and women, not the least of which is opening the way for this new generation of fathers. As a result of the commitment of men like those in this book, there is a growing recognition that men want to make their way home, to participate in society as parents as well as breadwinners. Despite the isolation they feel, it is becoming impossible to ignore the millions of men like them who are building a family life against tides of disbelief and disinterest and below the radar detection of statistics, trends, and (sadly) national policy.

When I began this book, I didn't know what I would feel about the men I would meet, but as I went along, I was persuaded by their earnestness and touched by their respect and adoration for their children. They weren't sure exactly why they were struggling to do things the way they were, and they were only vaguely aware of the societal pressures that were arrayed against them, but it was as if—for want of a better phrase, since this one is so rarely associated with men—"nurturing instinct" made them do it. That is why I am sure that they are not going to give up. That they are setting the stage for a national parents' agenda and building momentum for a revitalizing social change.

As the thousands of men—salesmen and factory workers, pilots and police officers, executives and clerks—grapple with the problems of confronting this new frontier, their efforts to create a balance between work and family will change family life. Whether they realize it or not, they are reinventing fatherhood.

FATHER COURAGE

CHAPTER ONE

WHAT'S GOING ON HERE?

The promise or threat that someday a boy might be called upon to give his life for his country has provided a historical setting for aspirations to heroism. At this moment in history, young males are in a particularly difficult spot, threatened with a world-wide catastrophe which no individual heroism can prevent and without a new means to exercise their biologically given aggressive protectiveness or desire for individual bravery. The necessary virtues of the present age are essentially domestic virtues, virtues that have long been regarded as more appropriate for women—patience, endurance, steadfastness. It is essential that the tasks of the future should be so organized that as dying for one's country becomes unfeasible, taking risks for that which is loved may still be possible.

—Margaret Mead, 1962
Introduction to *Male and Female*

1

SOME PEOPLE HATE LONG CAR TRIPS; Rick and Heather love them. They enjoy the opportunity to be in each other's company and away from the demands of the rest of their lives. They share the driving equally. She takes a couple of hours and then he takes over. The nondriving partner navigates, passes the water bottle, dozes. Rick is a very cautious driver; Heather goes for the max. Rick prefers the open road; Heather finds city traffic a challenge. Like all couples, they occasionally become exasperated with one another's driving style, but when it comes down to it, each trusts the other behind the wheel; each knows that the other would do nothing truly reckless. They like their system; it is fair and it is fun. There is never any question about who does more; Heather knows that Rick will do his share. Rick knows that he doesn't have to keep proving that. Why would he? They are a team.

Would that their other efforts at domestic job-sharing reflected as solid a partnership. Would that dividing up all family responsibilities were as precise a business as sharing the driving.

Far from it. As more couples set themselves the goal of "equal parenting" the more troublesome that phrase becomes; it hardly means the same thing to any two people let alone any two parents.

The same Heather and Rick who cruise America's highways in perfect harmony are out of alignment when it comes to their four-year-old daughter. Technically it is Rick's responsibility to get Betsy to day care in the morning, where she is picked up by a baby-sitter at two. Heather, who works flexible hours, usually gets home around five and cares for Betsy until Rick gets home around seven, when she gets dinner while Rick focuses on Betsy. Heather does the bath; Rick the bedtime story. Except when they don't.

Rick works long hours; Heather has a looser schedule—and makes a lot less money. When Rick has to go on a business trip—which is frequently—alternative arrangements have to be made for Betsy. Heather makes them, not Rick. And when Heather just can't manage dinner, they order in; Rick pays, but he doesn't take over KP. Rick is more involved in his daughter's life than his father was in his, and Heather has more freedom from child rearing than her mother did, but is this an equal parenting partnership? Do Heather and Rick think it is?

When I started this book I assumed that when men said they wanted to become full partners in their children's upbringing, and when women said it was about time that men did their share of child care, they were on the same page.

I looked at young parents like Heather and Rick as pioneers in a changed kind of marriage, coming as they do from a generation raised with a refined awareness of gender equity. They say "flight attendant" and "chairperson"; in college they lived in mixed dormitories; they dated in packs, not couples, and talked about career tracks with equal ambition. The men grew up aware of breakthroughs for women in politics and sports, and they were fully prepared for the possibility of working for a powerful woman. It was only logical that as these young people discussed marriage, they envisioned a shared workplace in the home, shared financial responsibilities, shared decision making, shared housework, and, often as an afterthought, shared child-rearing responsibilities.

This, I assumed, would be the generation that would begin the second stage of the gender-role revolution. This chapter would bring us in sight of the goal set out by early feminists: the social, economic, and political equality of men and women. In fact, it would parallel the first stage, the integration of women in the workplace, by bringing about the integration of men into family life. Indeed, it seemed instructive to look at the challenge the same way: just as women needed training and social support to make progress in the workplace, young fathers would need on-the-job training, mentoring, time-management skills, and a welcoming environment to help them learn the culture, while society at large would have to disabuse itself of certain gender stereotypes. Not easy, but perhaps easier than the first stage, because so much had already changed.

I envisioned a world transforming in a spirit of good faith and goodwill, as women helped men over the hurdle their sisters had confronted fifteen years earlier: the myth of "having it all." Having it all was once the double-edged sword that impaled many women who felt forced to pay for the permission to work with a flawless performance of their wife and mother roles—an effort clearly doomed to failure. No one can carry off two full-time jobs. What seemed on the surface to be encouragement for women to reach beyond traditional limitations was in reality a subtle punishment for overreaching, for wanting too much. But since then, due in part to societal acceptance and in part to economic pressures, the ambition of combining work and family has come to be a less punishable offense. This new generation of parents would, I imagined, demonstrate how to balance work and family, and their success would have an impact on both the workplace and the family that would, in turn, be reflected in national policy more supportive of American family life than it currently is.

My most fundamental assumption was that everyone shared an understanding of what fatherhood should be. After all, there are countless studies confirming that where fathers are actively involved in a warm relationship with their children, the children—from premature newborns to preschoolers to adolescents—thrive in childhood and prosper in later life. But who needs studies? The expression on a youngster's face at the sight of a beloved dad—and most dads are beloved, even neglectful ones—is study enough.

And what about the dad's expression? He would probably be embarrassed to see himself in such a moment of vulnerability and joy, but a snapshot of his face would supersede the mountain of research documenting how fatherhood enriches a man's spirit and brings a special kind of intimacy to his life.

A RUDE AWAKENING

It didn't take more than a few conversations about partnership for me to realize that while both parents might be hoping to affirm my assumptions and capture such joyous family moments, what one saw through the camera lens was almost always out of focus for the other. I saw it in the dismayingly frequent roll of the eyes from many of the women I asked about their husband's involvement. And I saw it in the men's enthusiastic but also sheepish accounts of their contributions. Overall, I found less goodwill than I had expected on the part of the individual partners and of society as well. For couples who had started out in closer harmony, the score changed dramatically when partnership became parenthood. Then, I found, support systems gave way, good intentions were not backed up by real commitment, frustration and bewilderment clouded the horizon.

MIKE AND DIANE—THE BEST LAID PLANS

Mike and Diane were both deeply committed to their careers when they got married five years ago, and for most of that time the security, support, and sheer fun of being married seemed to compound the enthusiasm they brought to their work. Their game plan had always included having children—both of them had grown up in large, warm families—and Diane got pregnant right on schedule. She worked through her pregnancy, up to the first labor pains, having arranged for everything she would need when the baby arrived. Her employer had a well-established maternity-leave policy, and she signed up for four months off. When Delia was born, Mike and Diane both expected to immerse themselves in caretaking. They both adored her. But Diane was there, and Mike was not. Soon most of the tending to Delia's needs fell to Diane, so did most of the bonding; playtime and walks with Delia nestled in her Snugli and an increasingly fine-tuned connection with the baby became second nature to her. The same experiences became special occasions for Mike, whose work was as demanding as ever in terms of both time and attention.

At this point in the story, one might expect to hear about Diane's resentment of Mike's unbroken career track, his freedom to come and go in child care, his lack of understanding of what her day was like. But that is not the story. In fact, Diane was very happy to return from maternity leave to a three-day workweek at a less high-powered version of her old job. She had made her peace with what she saw as necessary trade-offs between the drive toward an all-systems-go career trajectory and the pleasures and demands of parenthood.

It was Mike who was resentful and conflicted. He had looked forward to the egalitarian family life he and Diane had dreamed about; he expected to be there for the serendipitous and mundane moments of parenting; he hated being a guest in his baby's world.

He was also beginning to feel anxious about his job. Was he concentrating as intensely as before? Was he shortchanging the team-spirit time with his bosses in order to get home sooner? Was he losing his edge—and the guarantee of financial success? And why was it that Diane seemed to have all the luck, including the intimacy with the baby that he missed, the job satisfaction, the domesticity he felt too wired to enjoy. To his horror, Mike realized that he was angry at Diane because she seemed to be having it all and he couldn't.

Instead of becoming the involved family man of his game plan, he was turning into the sort of bring-home-the-bacon guy, like his own father, whose half a life he had dismissed as unacceptable. What's more, although he hated having to devote so much time and attention to his work, at least he was good at that job, and getting better. When it came to his other job, coparenting, he seemed to be losing ground. He was regularly confronted with his total ineptness in domestic duties: the fact that in newlywed days he could cook up a storm didn't mean much when faced with his inability to cope with a cranky infant. It seemed as though all his sources of satisfaction had been injected with several drops of vinegar. But

Mike is determined to concentrate on the nectar of those moments with Delia and Diane that are everything he hoped for. He is not discouraged; he sees his predicament as the growing pains of a new kind of family man.

THE OTHER HALF OF THE EQUATION

As much as the women they are married to are delighted at the prospect of a more committed and sharing partner, they are experiencing their share of setbacks and surprises. As social historian John R. Gillis points out, "The reimaging of fatherhood cannot take place in the absence of a reconsideration of motherhood."

Diane's view of family life shifted as much as Mike's did during those early months of parenting; her expectations have changed in ways she didn't anticipate. As she became increasingly pleased with herself as a mother and more adept at handling the many demands of a small child, she found that what she wanted from Mike had changed. The more expert she became at managing their domestic life, the less she wanted to share the experience; when Mike tried to do things on his own initiative, he only seemed to get in the way. If the truth were known, she would rather he took his orders from her and helped out when and how she wants him to.

Yet that setup codifies the inequities and is a regular source of annoyance. When she asks Mike to pick up something from the store, he occasionally forgets, and when he comes home, he seems to think that his only obligation in family management is to spend time with Delia. If his view of his role in the family can be described as fathering and, to give the modern partner his due, husbanding, hers is everything else. That is her burden; it is also her power.

As long as she is calling the shots, she is not betraying her time-honored role as keeper of the flame. As long as he is helping, she is freed from the limitations of the maternal role and able to function in the world of grown-ups. But making this less-than-equal-but-more-than-traditional system work calls for great efficiency. Under time pressure, the one with the expertise becomes the micromanager. There is simply no time to do anything—from bathing the baby to loading the dishwasher—any other way than by what men have come to call "Mommy's Rules."

My favorite illustration of Mommy's Rules in action occurs in an episode of the television sitcom *Home Improvement*. Tim, as he frequently does, tries to take on some household duties, claiming that anybody who knows how to handle tools and clean up after a lube job can handle housework; typically he ends up blowing up some household appliance and retreating chagrined to his workroom. This time Jill, his wife, is explaining the Sponge Ritual to him: New sponges are used only for dishes; when you introduce a new sponge, you move its predecessor down a notch to countertop cleaner, and the one before it moves down to everything-else cleaner.

I am sure every woman watching had a similar reaction to mine—yes, that's right, that's the way I do it; I am also sure that most men reacted the way Tim did, with bewilderment and a dismissive grunt. The mysteries of Eleusis couldn't be more inscrutable to the noninitiated than the Sponge Ritual must seem to most men.

Tim's benighted domestic status has ironic parallels to the position of the breakthrough executive woman of twenty years ago—condescended to, excluded from key pieces of information, and never able to escape the watchful eye of a supervisor. In other words, second-class citizens, not full partners.

In a further irony, Mommy's Rules also describes the situation in many workplaces with respect to parents. In this context, it is the rules for "Mommies Only." In both cases, men have less of a voice than they may want.

Recent surveys show growing adoption of family-friendly policies including parental leave, flexible work hours, and cafeteria benefits in response to demands by both women and men for a balance between the pull of work and of home. In theory, the options are there for men and women. In practice, though, it is primarily women who are societally and professionally encouraged and supported in their efforts, while men are still considered suspect if they express interest in taking advantage of family benefits. Routinely men who want to take time off for the birth of a child are urged sotto voce to take vacation or sick leave, not the still stigmatized "paternity leave."

It is clear to those new fathers that their fraternity looks down on their choice. So they are embarrassed and their friends, who are picking up the same message, are embarrassed for them. And what do most men do when they are confused and embarrassed? Clam up. More than any other theme that has emerged from my interviews, the lack of openness among men about parenting and family life is stunning.

WHO CAN YOU TRUST?

Most men admit that they are mistrustful of other men; they envy the intimacy of women's friendships. Conversations about the taping episode of the Monica Lewinsky scandal were illuminating in this respect (perhaps only in this respect): women of all political stripes were outraged by the way the young woman's confidence had been betrayed by her friend Linda Tripp. As several feminist commentators pointed out, women use intimate conversations with friends to think out loud, to explore problems in a safe environment. That safety is sacrosanct in women's culture. And Linda

Tripp violated the code. Men, on the other hand, were not at all surprised at what happened to Lewinsky. Over and over I heard how they wouldn't dream of confiding anything that could be used against them, such as doubt, failure, even illness. It is no surprise, then, that they can't find a safe haven among other men for addressing a life experience that is the focus of so much private and public ambivalence as fatherhood.

Instead, they have learned to count on women to penetrate the impersonal evasions that they often hide behind and translate emotions into manageable units; women can make a risky topic safe and mitigate shame and awkwardness with camaraderie and humor. One father admitted that the only time he can open up about parenting pressures and worries with other fathers is in couples, when the women "facilitate" the discussion, or when he is talking to his women friends. Another told me that he and his closest friends count on one another's wives to alert them when their husbands are in trouble or need a little male TLC.

The end result is that whatever instruction—or encouragement, for that matter—that a father gets on domestic life is going to be from his wife and, through her, from her friends and her magazines (men's magazines are, if anything, anti-family in their celebration of narcissism and the single life). Like the Sponge Ritual, parenting advice is built on the

Mommy model, which for many men fits just about as well as Cinderella's slipper fit her stepsisters.

DEAR OLD DAD

The contemporary father has no personal history of Daddy models to draw on. All but a lucky few of the men I spoke to mourned the absence of fathering in their childhoods. Curiously, many reported being golf orphans, resentful children left behind on Saturday morning when the dad they had hardly seen all week abandoned them again—by choice this time, not necessity. Many told of being frightened of a father's unpredictable temper; others sensed that their fathers disapproved of them. Not one man I spoke to wanted to be the same kind of father he had had.

Yet, alienated as a man may feel from the tradition that has brought him to this point in time, it is not easy to shed generations of assumptions about men as stolid family providers and sometime warriors.

If the Barbie doll embodies a limited image of women, G.I. Joe is the male counterpart. War toys and action figures commemorate an exaggerated image of manhood that has been held up to generations of men even as circumstances changed. The original G.I.s returned home from World War II to a grateful nation and were rewarded with an education (on the G.I. Bill) and a job (the women who had done much of the war work were called upon to relinquish their paychecks to a more deserving man). National policy was clear: the war winners of the forties were to be transformed into the breadwinners of the fifties.

The breadwinners' sons, in turn, grew up to a very different kind of war, Vietnam. Public misgivings over that war discredited the soldier-hero side of the traditional male self-image. Yet, for their generation, the breadwinner role held firm. Now, *their* sons are being forced to relinquish that role, too, by economic circumstances.

One income is rarely enough to support a family, and even if it were, any single paycheck is precarious in a marketplace where loyalty and job security are increasingly meaningless. Even more unsettling, according to economist Sylvia Ann Hewlett and Harvard professor Cornel West, authors of *The War Against Parents*, over the last twenty-five years "wages have fallen much faster for men than for women, and young men have suffered disproportionately. Since 1973, wages are down 25 percent for men aged 25 to 34, and the pace of decline has quickened since 1990. The implications for family life," Hewlett and West conclude, "are dire: more work, lower pay and less time for children."

In another blow to the heroic-provider image, men find themselves sharing wage-earning status with women and occasionally even taking second place. For some, it is a distressing and even humiliating experience. An engineer told a *Ladies' Home Journal* focus group that he had finally come up with the perfect rejoinder to teasing from his coworkers: "Other engineers, some of the older guys, would say: 'Doesn't it make you mad that your wife earns more than you?' I said, 'I don't know. Does it make you mad that my wife earns more than *you*?'"

Unseated by these major economic shifts, today's family man can't see himself as a war winner or a breadwinner; measured by the standards of generations past, he is a no-winner.

Perhaps on some level, the urgency of the longing for family life is taking the place of the breadwinner's devotion to (financial) security and the war winner's sense of moral purpose. As a calling, fatherhood—as men are redefining it—summons up the virtues of dedication, self-sacrifice, loyalty, and cooperation. Although the work is often hard and tedious, the payoff couldn't be richer, much richer, in fact, than any that the breadwinner or the war winner actually could experience.

For more and more men the pull toward parenting is intense, and whether or not the men who say they are trying to become more fully engaged in family life are getting anywhere near achieving it, most claim to be profoundly committed. The harder they try, though, the sooner they learn that they are up against some formidable disincentives to persevere.

BARRIERS AND BEWILDERMENT

In the workplace, for example, the choice—if there is one—seems to be between a corps of driven achievers who value work over family and a band of wimpy foot soldiers on a career track to nowhere. At home, the choice seems to be equally unappealing, between becoming "Mr. Mom" or being typecast as a chronic slacker who doesn't do his share.

One measure of those pressures is the amount of stress they engender. When James Levine, the longtime crusader for recognition of the plight of "working fathers," lectures, he begins by posing a pair of questions about work-family conflicts. First, he asks the working mothers in the audience to rate the degree of stress they feel on a scale of one to ten. Most rate it in the eights, nines, and tens. Then he asks the working fathers to rate their stress, and lo and behold, the fathers are up there in the eights and nines and tens, too. Levine uses this exercise to prove that the concern of fathers is not sufficiently recognized in the culture at large. In his book *Working Fathers,* he argues that "one of the common denominators among working fathers is feeling torn by two emotions: guilt for not spending more time with their children and worry about being able to make a living."

Levine's anecdote dramatizes the degree of stress both parents are under; it also suggests how stress gets compounded. As in Mike and Diane's story, his failings not only cause him guilt, but are a source of her stress. And her resentment is stressful right back.

DON: "OOPS, I FORGOT—AGAIN"

Don and his wife, Beverly, seem to have the most synergistic parenting setup imaginable. He has the flexibility of an academic's hours and a generous parental leave policy; she is a book editor with equally family-friendly benefits. Beverly took three months of leave right after Sam was born; Don took the next semester off and cared for him when she went back to work. They spend equal amounts of time on household responsibilities and probably spend equal amounts of time with Sam. Don's description of his days with the baby made clear he wasn't faking it—he described not only the ecstasy of bonding but the agony of boredom; like millions of devoted caregivers, a high point of his day was getting out of the house on errands.

So when I asked Don whether he thought Beverly would say he does his share, I was pretty sure he would say yes (even if she wouldn't). He did say yes, but it was a very tentative yes, accompanied by a sheepish grin. "Well, except for one thing," he added. "She hates that she has to tell me everything I have to do." Preparing the daily bag lunch for their son is the example that came to his mind. "I know he needs a lunch every day, and I don't mind at all making it, but I won't think of it until she reminds me. That drives her crazy."

I can imagine her crying out in exasperation, "But he needs his lunch every day! How can you not think of it? What part of lunch is it you don't understand!" And I can see by the expression on Don's face that he feels he has been naughty but in a kind of winning and mischievous way.

We talked a little about what it means to have to keep track of everything the way Beverly does, to live with what I later began to call the "Dreaded Tape." Don recognized the concept, admitting that he has a tape going in his own mind about his work; Beverly does, too, he pointed out. When I suggested that for her the work tape is on the same reel as the Dreaded Tape, he conceded that that made a big difference. Now that he got the picture, would he be ready to take on tape duty? He was evasive. "Well, I do feel guilty—to fall back on a cliché—because I know it upsets her. My response is not so much, 'Gee, I really wish I could change and remember to make the lunch'; my response is basically about her, not about me."

Deafness to the rat-a-tat-tat of the Dreaded Tape on the part of men explains why, for example, a study showing that father participation in home life is up dramatically that was reported in the *New York Times* on April 15 was followed on April 16 by a response from an indignant woman; she questioned the validity of the self-measured statistics and cited other studies that show that it is almost exclusively mothers who go to PTA meetings. To the average reader the complaint may sound a tad mean-spirited, but it goes to the heart of the rolling eyes I encountered when I began asking about involved fathers. The fact of the matter is that no matter how many hours the fathers put into sharing the work of family life, as long as the responsibility for seeing that the job is done is not shared, it will never be enough.

Explanations for the growth of this third eye when women become mothers and the blind spot that afflicts their husbands at exactly the same time are many and inconclusive. Some are physiological, having to do with gender differences in brain patterns; some are behavioral, based on men's preference for concentrating on one thing at a time, while women are more adept at multitasking; some are cultural, the deep-seated assumptions on the part of both men and women that women are divinely endowed with mysterious gifts and intuitions that make them better equipped for family life. Political explanations go to the question of who has more power, the person giving the orders or the person refusing to do a task until asked.

The question here is not whether there are two parents in the picture, but whether there is a primary parent calling the shots. When a man is a single parent he usually develops that "third eye" and becomes as adept as any mother at handling the job. That should be encouraging news to men who claim they are intimidated by the "maternal instinct."

What it all comes down to—the ball of yarn tangled around the ankles of even generously supportive couples—is that most women are convinced that most men have no idea what it really takes to be an involved parent. Most men, in turn, have few opportunities to demonstrate on their own terms what they might mean by their desire to be one.

The notion that for men to become—and remain—involved fathers all that is needed is some remedial diapering doesn't begin to address the problem. The truth is that we don't really know what it is that men need to learn or even how they would best learn it.

Most disconcerting of all, we don't really know how much their kind of parenting would look like mothering. And how women would react if it didn't.

JAMES—GHOST STORIES AND INSTINCT

James struck me as a father who had moved way beyond Parenting 101. When I interviewed him, I was very taken by how comfortable he seemed with the nitty-gritty of daily parenting and household management. He knew, for example, that if you kept the heel of the bread in the bag with the rest of the loaf, the loaf would stay fresher; laughingly he told me how his wife had originally thought he was leaving the heel because he was a picky eater. His comfort seemed to be due to plenty of experience and a very flexible lifestyle. He and his wife, Fiona, had an enviably fluid work history: sometimes he works, sometimes she works, and they shift whenever the mood or the financial pressure strikes them. He talked a lot about following his instinct as a parent and how he learned to trust in that instinct. I took note of this insight; it sounded like an important one.

By way of illustration, he told me about how out of place he feels in the mothers' culture, particularly parents' groups at school. Also, he said, sometimes they don't understand his parenting style. He had several calls from mothers of his kids' friends dismayed by a story his two sons were telling. James, it seems, had told them that seven of their predecessors who hadn't listened to their dad are buried in the backyard. He doesn't see what all the fuss is about; he knows kids like scary stories and he is absolutely sure that they know he made this one up.

I was as shocked by this ghoulish anecdote as the mothers who called to protest. It was hard not to rush to the judgment that James's "instinct" is a menace to all the children in the neighborhood. Maybe, though, it is especially easy to rush to that judgment for women raised on a litany of ways children needed to be protected from men. Well versed in examples of male violence, abandonment, and abuse of power, we find it hard to wholeheartedly accept and trust a specific man with our children. Even if they are his children, too, and he is the most devoted and knowledgeable father in all respects.

And what if James's instincts really *are* "wrong"? Might he not benefit from the input of other men who can help him understand why, rather than the censure of women who can't imagine what possesses a man to tell a story like that?

We won't know if differences in parenting behavior are nurture or nature—or both—until enough men and women have put a more egalitarian approach into practice. It is too much to ask of one generation. But when the pioneers in blending work and family hand the world over to their children, it is certain that parenting will be a very different enterprise.

THE GLASS HALF FULL

The transformation of parenting is going to involve redefining the terms we use to measure our life experience. "Success," for example, is used primarily in connection with work; it could apply to family life, too; or "equality," which describes a measurable kind of sharing that may more realistically give way to something more complex that might be termed "equity." The transformation is also going to involve reconsidering the ways families work. Can two people divide up the responsibility—the items on her Dreaded Tape, from the need for butter to the timing of flu shots to the emotional pulse-taking of every member of the family—as well as the chores? If not, is there a way to install a boss who is more acceptable than the classic authority figure? Until we are all speaking from the same lexicon when we talk about parenting, until we are working with a more accurate—and more flexible—job description, we will have trouble addressing the imbalances that exist outside individual families.

A lot is at stake here, because unless family-friendly policies result in professional satisfaction *and* respect for parents, the private struggles alone will not achieve balance. Public values can't continue to be at odds with private ones. We can only hope that the momentum that can grow out of a more wholesome cooperation in the family structure will pick up steam in the workplace and build from there into a national referendum on family policy.

Shaping the public conversation is probably the hardest part of the equation. Not only do many of the powers-that-be in our daily lives work against the good instincts of the emerging band of involved fathers, but by their standards such efforts are not even noteworthy. The measure of events is whether they are "news." News is what happens on the battlefields and in the halls of power, not in the kitchen. Men make news in the world, not in the home. News is about conflict; family life is about cooperation among busy, burdened people trying to get through the day. News is about crime and punishment; parenting is about flawed but well-meaning behavior that calls for understanding and support. News is about winners and losers; family life is about not giving up, because you simply can't.

No wonder, then, despite their numbers, stories of fathers struggling to remake their world don't show up often enough on the public radar screen.

This book tells the stories of real people living this change, in the hope that their experiences will resonate with those of the unacknowledged community of like-minded souls out there. Armed with the knowledge that they are not alone and with insight into what is going on with their wives and partners, those men may find a clearer understanding of what is happening to them. And what courage it takes to persevere against personal, professional, political, and social odds, to succeed as well as fail. "We all have character traits which make us less than perfectly parental," writes Dorothy Dinnerstein, a groundbreaking thinker about gender issues, in *The Mermaid and The Minotaur.* "What is not faced head-on is the fact that under present conditions woman does not share man's right to have such traits without loss of human stature, and man does not share woman's obligations to work at mastering them."

As the fathers whose stories I have listened to gain understanding and confidence, they will, I hope, be galvanized to press for change with enhanced conviction, keeping in mind that although we can't win all the battles, we just may win the war.

CHAPTER TWO

Sons of Distant Fathers

My child arrived just the other day
He came to the world in the usual way
But there were planes to catch and bills to pay
He learned to walk while I was away
And he was talkin' 'fore I knew it
And as he grew, he'd say,
"I'm gonna be like you, Dad
You know I'm gonna be like you"

> *And the cat's in the cradle and the silver spoon*
> *Little boy blue and the man in the moon*
> *When you comin' home, Dad?*
> *I don't know when, but we'll get together then*
> *You know we'll have a good time then*

My son turned ten just the other day
He said, "Thanks for the ball, Dad, c'mon, let's play
Can you teach me to throw?" I said, "Not today

I got a lot to do," he said, "That's OK"
And he walked away but his smile never dimmed
It said, "I'm gonna be like him, yeah
You know I'm gonna be like him"

•   •   •   •   •   •   •   •   •   •

I've long since retired, my son's moved away
I called him up just the other day
I said, "I'd like to see you if you don't mind"
He said, "I'd love to, Dad, if I can find the time
You see, my new job's a hassle and the kids have the flu
But it's sure nice talkin' to you, Dad
It's been sure nice talkin' to you"
And as I hung up the phone, it occurred to me
He'd grown up just like me
My boy was just like me
—Harry and Sandra Chapin, "Cat's in the Cradle," 1974

"CAT'S IN THE CRADLE" was a hit when most of the men in this book were toddlers. In its lament for lost opportunity, their fathers recognized a relationship they didn't want to repeat; yet if the now grown-up sons are to be believed, their fathers did not escape the curse of growing up "just like" their own disconnected fathers.

Over and over again I heard rueful recollections like this one from Conrad: "I never—until the day he died, until he was dead actually—told him that I loved him and I don't remember him ever telling me that." Or Paul's: "We were kind of temperamentally different; he was like type A workaholic. And I didn't see him that much, and I took it personally. I thought, Oh, he doesn't like me." Paul saw a particular rival for his father's attention in the Saturday golf game. "I remember being very young, he'd be off to work very early in the morning, come home late, for a kid relatively late. So I don't remember seeing him very much. I have this one memory of waking up on a Saturday morning, and I said to my mom, 'Where's Dad?' And she's like, 'Oh, he's off playing golf.' And I was like, 'Well, doesn't he want to see me?' I remember feeling very hurt. Then he would come back from golf and take a nap. And if, God forbid, me or my sister made any noise, he'd scream. It was scary, like walking on eggshells."

As these sons become fathers themselves, they are consciously setting a different course for themselves. But while the goal—a balance between work and family, between the contribution of husband and wife—is easy to define, the path is very, very hard to travel without the inner map of experience. For one thing, the only guidance most have from their own parents is the negative pole of their fathers' behavior, and from their mothers, an inverted picture of the work/family struggle ahead of them.

They want to trade the entitlement of a Saturday golf game and the power to make their children quake in their shoes for fluency in the vocabulary of love. They want to "be there" for their children in all ways, even if that means sacrificing certain economic and professional goals, personal pastimes, a degree of authority, and more than a degree of dignity. Like the women of their mothers' generation, they are lashing themselves to the mast, finding little support and some hostility, as they try to navigate the seas of balancing love and work.

Paul's childhood snapshot embodies a cautionary image: "It was a very traditional family, so my mother would be the one who would kind of plan the activities, and take care of the kids, deal with school, make the lunches, go to the PTA meetings. I very rarely remember my father doing that with my mother. Maybe once or twice. He sort of made the bread, and she kind of ran the family. He wasn't really big on just the day-to-day raising of us, where I really intend to be. I really want to do that."

The closest Paul came to becoming a part of his father's life was when his parents separated for two years, and his father had to figure out parenting on his own. "It was very traumatic for the family, but it was really great for my relationship with my father, because suddenly we saw each other on weekends, and he got really affectionate, which was wonderful. I'd sit in his lap and then he'd play with us more. I think he was really bad at things like that at first. But he kind of learned. When they went back together, we fell back into the same old pattern. So I sort of lost him again for many years."

Paul is determined that his son will never lose his father that way.

HOW THE DADS GOT LOST

A vision of new family roles was shaped over the past forty years by social, economic, and historical forces as well as individual domestic dramas. The post-war emergence of American prestige in the world and the increasing experience with political security and economic prosperity at home laid the groundwork. But the energy for change came from the several social movements of the sixties and seventies— civil rights, feminism, human potential—that preached equal opportunity and personal growth and denounced the hierarchical, patriarchal, capitalist model. The model that Dear Old Dad was built for.

Until then, throughout this century, the broad-stroke shape of family life had been the increasing physical and emotional separation of dad from the rest of the family and the increasing pressure on him, and him alone, to be the breadwinner.

That trend began when the industrial revolution transformed the family from a unit with various working parts— both parents generally worked the same soil or shop and were visible if not attentive to their children around the clock—into a refuge for the one weary wage earner. The father was, for all intents and purposes, banished from the household, and his work itself became a distant mystery to the rest of the family. He lost the companionship of his family and the satisfaction of passing on what he knew to his sons. What he gained was a regular paycheck and the recognition that he was providing for his family... or not.

When the Depression threw a generation of men out of work in the 1930s, the entire family was cut loose from the economic system. The crisis confirmed, in its ruination of so many men, the importance of the breadwinner and the singularity of his burden.

If the distance between home and workplace needed any more of a wedge, the mobilization for war that took place in the forties sealed the issue. Soon the men who had been going off to work, were going off to war. And not coming home for supper. Millions of children spent three fatherless years, and millions more never got to know their fathers at all. The war-weary men who came home were unrecognizable to their families, and their families were just as unrecognizable to them.

For one thing, their wives had become the decision makers and often the breadwinners. An enormous propaganda machine called upon their patriotism to get women out of the house and into the factories and steel plants where they were desperately needed. The push was backed up with the pull of publicly funded on-site child-care facilities, which enabled women to taste the satisfaction of combining motherhood and gainful employment. At war's end, it took an even more massive program to get women out of the jobs that "rightfully belonged" to men, but even as most women reluctantly withdrew, the experience was not lost on them—or their children. They had become women of the world, used to earning and managing money, and their children had become children of the world, used to a community of their peers and answerable to teachers and mothers, not only male authority figures.

The reentry process was, of course, even harder on the men. The war was a sobering but also a liberating adventure for those 12 million young soldiers, who had been uprooted from all they knew and thrown into the midst of much they never expected to know. In 1946, the popular movie *The Best Years of Our Lives* captured the confusion many returning vets experienced when they confronted the contrast between what had been expected of them in Europe or the Pacific and what was expected of them back home. As the Fredric March character put it in a burst of frustration, "Last year it was 'Kill Japs!' Now it's 'Make money!'"

His country offered support to the veteran who wanted a job or an education—and a home in the suburbs. But as he resumed his position at the head of his family, the working father found himself setting off in one direction to capture a piece of the postwar prosperity while his family went off in another to "enjoy" it. His work was so distant and irrelevant that the idealized television father Ozzie Nelson (the Nelsons of *Ozzie and Harriet* were the best-known television family of the fifties) didn't need to be given a specific job to make him seem "real." Dad had become his paycheck.

"When I was a little kid," humorist Erma Bombeck recalls, "a father was like the light in the refrigerator. Every house had one, but no one really knew what either of them did once the door was shut."

Meanwhile, the suburban wife of the American Dream was polishing that refrigerator and looking through magazines for news of the "new, improved" model. In reality, she often found herself removed from any possibility of outside work, in an economic system where her job was not earning, but spending. Her isolated and overprotected existence became "the problem that has no name" identified by Betty Friedan in 1963. The movement to break out emerged in the sixties along with the other rebellions that had one thing in common: the demand for more life rather than more things. Paycheck Dad became the embodiment of all that was wrong.

The civil rights movement, the anti–Vietnam War protests, the counterculture ("sex, drugs, and rock 'n' roll") all carried a similar message: don't trust anyone over thirty, and don't trust anyone of any age in authority. It was very hard for any father—or mother, for that matter—to reach his (or her) kids, even if the intimacy and family experience had been there to start with.

"I don't know what you were doing in the late Sixties," writes journalist Mark Hunter in an effort to counter what he calls "the Distant Father fad" with a wash of reality, "but I was driving my father out of the house with an electric guitar he bought me, smoking pot, making love with my girlfriend under his roof—hey, you think he felt jealous?—and telling him and his friends every chance I got that they were square, wrong, doomed, along with the rest of the Establishment. So was every self-respecting guy I knew. We were revolutionaries, man. Thus I find it slightly weird when guys who sank their fangs in Daddy's hand complain that he didn't stroke them enough."

Over the next decade, the head of the household was fairly well decapitated. (Indeed the term "head of household" was removed from the Census Bureau's population survey in 1980, under pressure from the women's movement to find terminology that reflected partnership.) The sense of security that a father figure—the light in the refrigerator—represented was rendered as meaningless as everything else that had been held sacred. More compelling were news stories about delinquent fathers—"deadbeat dads"—who shirked their responsibilities to provide security for their children or those who brought violence into the home. By the late nineties, the headlines were about Census Bureau findings that "nearly one-fourth (24 percent) of America's children lived in mother-only families" which translates into 17 million children living in families with no father present.

Even if the former "head of household" was still in the household, he was less and less the head of it, even in terms of earning power. As the economic boom of the 1980s deflated, many men were left facing layoffs and cutbacks and bankruptcies where they had been building financial security. They could "no longer count on their careers as unquestioned source of self-fulfillment—or even as a clear path to financial success," reported sociologist Michael Kimmel in the *Harvard Business Review*. By the early 1980s they were hearing from demographers that they were the first U.S. generation to be less financially successful than their fathers were at the same age. "This economic decline," concludes Kimmel, "has caused many men to reevaluate work in a harsh new light."

And, one might add, to reevaluate family life in a warm new light.

Warm it may be, but it is not the clear light of day. As we have seen, the father of the nineties has very little to draw on in the way of personal experience or role models. His wife is no better equipped to fill in the blanks; after all she had the same kind of father he did. And she shares some underlying assumptions with him.

Susan Faludi argues, in her book *Stiffed: The Betrayal of the American Man,* that men are dismayed to find that even those who support their efforts to shed their "macho" past, are sending a double message. "Both the feminist and anti-feminist views," she writes, "are rooted in a peculiarly modern American perception that to be a man means you are at the controls at all times. The popular feminist joke that men are to blame for everything is the flip side of the 'family values' reactionary expectation that men should be in charge of everything."

So, while men and women both have only a vague sense of what they mean by an egalitarian family life, that fantasy is shaped by the cultural conversation going on around them. Any discussion about family life, including the father's role, is for the most part shaped by women's vision. It remains for the men who are trying to combine love and work to live a model that speaks in a male voice.

There is some evidence that this new voice is emerging. Don Conway-Long, a son of the sixties, who has been teaching a Men and Masculinity course to undergraduates since 1980 at Washington University in St. Louis, sees a change in his students. "I started out teaching kind of on the edge of my own generation, and now I'm on to a complete new one.

At the edge—at the end of mine—the men in particular had much more of a sense of being angry at their fathers and being father-wounded, which is basically a huge part of my generation's talk, which is where we get all that Bly nonsense—the missing dad, the empty spot where he should have been sort of thing." Nowadays, he told me, "a higher percentage of them have what they consider to be good relationships with their fathers. Which means that my generation of men seem to have gotten it together somewhat."

That should be of some encouragement to the men I interviewed, because most of them, when asked to be specific about the kind of father they want to be, responded in almost identical terms: "not like mine."

CONRAD—"A SIDE OF HIM I NEVER SAW"

Conrad, a dark-haired and brooding man in his early forties, seems permanently coiled, always on the alert as he must have had to be during years he roamed the world as a foreign correspondent. Yet he is also soft-spoken and thoughtful, especially when he speaks of his two children, Peter, who is eleven, and Jane, who is eight. He and his wife, Mary, live in a cluttered apartment that reflects the needs of both generations that live there; the sofa is flanked by one large rocking chair and one minia-

ture one. Although Conrad grew up in Britain, his experience was typical of the more alienated sons of distant fathers.

"MY DAD DIED THIS YEAR so this has all been quite fresh to me. He was an amazingly uncommunicative man, a very sweet, gentle, passive, quiet, self-effacing, rather incompetent man. He was very nice, but he was not a father who inspired a lot of complex memories about fathering. About fifteen years ago, when I went into therapy briefly, the first conversation was, 'What were your first memories of your father,' and I said, 'Standing in the potato patch in our garden, both digging in silence, and me, counting in my head, to infinity.'

"He was very hands-off. He went to the office. My mother was in very poor health for most of my childhood, and she was in the hospital a lot. I remember him not coping very well; she would cook meals for a week before she went into the hospital, so he didn't have to think about anything. He almost, literally, could not boil an egg.

"I remember being very upset at the things he couldn't do. He was an undereducated, bright fellow who, given a different trajectory, might have accomplished a lot, I suspect. But he wasn't mechanically adept; he wasn't physically adept. He wasn't athletic.

"We had a good, healthy, nice, civilized family. I can remember on one hand the times I heard my father raise his voice. I can remember once in my life hearing him use the word 'damn.' It was on that level of kind of restraint and politeness. Everyone said the same thing when he died, 'He was a decent, good, solid, reliable, man with integrity'—that was the word everyone used—but very passive with it.

"My father was given a model of fathering from his father, which was appalling. My grandfather was a small-town cop in Scotland and he was very narrow and very rigid and very unaffectionate. He was one of those rural, conservative guys who didn't believe in education for his children—if he left school at twelve that was good enough for them—and all this kind of stuff.

"So I think my dad had very low self-esteem, and I never heard him articulate what he thought he was on the planet for, what he thought he was a father for, or what anything else was about. He just went through the day and came out the other end and lived eighty-four years and kicked off and that was that.

"Golf was his passion; I went through a period of getting lessons for my birthday when I was about fourteen and then decided after about a month that this really wasn't for me, and I think that probably broke his heart.

"He belonged to a golf club, and for the better part of thirty years or more, he was really a fixture of a little clique of guys, several of whom were much younger than he was. Probably the youngest of the group weren't that much older than me. They really, really adored him and they kind of teased him and he was this quiet, serene, sort of self-effacing guy, who would never drink very much; he'd sit in the corner and be very shy. He was the elder statesman. But he was a man of very, very few words. They really liked him. Again, maybe they saw a side of him I never saw.

"He was a very sweet and loving grandfather, which makes me mistrust my memory a little bit. I suppose part of it is that things had changed, the world had changed and it was forty or more years later, but part of it is that he was actually very physically expressive with my kids, more than I can ever recall him being with any-one else. He would be very physical and have them on his knees and read them stories and I suppose he must have done those things for me, but the odd thing is I just don't remember them.

"The logical question would be, 'Well, didn't you talk to him about that stuff? Didn't you talk to him about how grandfathering was as opposed to parenting?' and the fact of the matter was that we never had a vocabulary for dealing with that stuff."

Despite his own disappointments, Conrad seems to have managed to achieve the intimacy with his children that he so desperately sought. He evoked that intense bonding more effectively than almost anyone else I interviewed when he described one day several years earlier when his son, Peter, was sick.

"He had had like seven ear infections in a row, and he got this thing where he just threw up all the time—and on that day we just got more and more covered in vomit, and stuck together closer and closer, and in the end I gave up changing clothes and we just sort of spent the day covered in vomit. It was the most wonderful day. It was this feeling of just absolute closeness, like when you go out in the rain and get so wet that you put your umbrella down, because it doesn't matter if you get any wetter, and you just feel completely liberated by it."

PAUL—"DAD WAS GOING THROUGH HIS OWN THINGS"

Paul, thirty-four, a filmmaker, was not yet a father when I first spoke to him. He lives in Connecticut with his wife, Beth, an academic. When she become pregnant seven months earlier, he decided to begin keeping a journal about his feelings as he moved toward becoming a par-

ent. His unlined baby face concentrated in earnestness as he described his dreams and apprehensions. When I asked him if any themes had emerged in his entries, his answer was instantaneous.

"IT'S FUNNY YOU SHOULD ASK. The biggest theme for the first six months was my own relationship to my father—which was shocking to me. Because I thought it would be about what I wanted to be as a parent. But then it sort of all crystallized and it was all kind of about how I felt I would have liked certain things from my father that I didn't get.

"He was going through his own things, but as a kid you don't realize that. He was in a family business, and I guess dealing with his own father. I don't think he had really emotionally separated from his father until his father died, which was when I was about twenty-six. I started getting closer to him then; once his father died, it freed him up.

"Until then, I think he saw himself more as a son than a father. I mean, he was a good provider, and he was there as a father, but I don't think he saw himself as a father.

"I felt that I was sort of a freak in his eyes because he was very much business oriented and I was very much into photography and kind of a spacey kid. It was difficult for him to understand where I was coming from and he was wondering what I would end up like, I don't know, artsy-fartsy. I was also a terrible athlete as a kid. (I've gotten much better at that, thankfully.) So there's definitely this homophobic aspect to it. I kind of remember him one time telling me I shouldn't hold my hand like this—it was just sort of hanging out. So there was definitely this element of you've got to be macho.

"Then I went through my rebellious teen years; I grew my hair long, and was smoking lots of dope. I was pissing him off, and coming home late and sleeping late. He couldn't understand my rebellion, which I think is really healthy—you need to have your kids sort of hate you for a few years, and then they come back.

"I remember a turning point. I must have been in my mid-twenties already—and I was going through some kind of personal crisis after college. I didn't know what to do. I felt like I was sort of wandering around and kind of groundless. I felt a lot of pressure from my parents like, well, go get some kind of job. My relationship with him just got worse and worse; he was very critical and biting and not very helpful because he just doesn't have that ability to say, 'Well, gee, you have this sort of temperament, I think you should get this kind of job.' Then—all of a sudden—he finally did. He said, 'Well, since you do video, why don't you videotape weddings?' And I said, 'Sure.' And that really worked out well."

DON—"I WAS ALWAYS A LITTLE SCARED OF HIM"

Don was among the happiest fathers I spoke to. At thirty-two, he loves his work—he's a professor of political science—and adores the life he and his wife have built around their four-year-old son, Sam. He looks back on his four months of paternity leave with realism about the tedium and pleasure at the intimacy. When I asked him if he felt he had both of Freud's requirements for happiness—love and work—he answered an enthusiastic yes. But the energy went out of his voice when he talked about his own father.

HE CHARACTERIZED THEIR RELATIONSHIP as "the normal father-son stuff, like Little League"—despite his father's chronic ill health. He was pretty sure his father's work "wasn't what he pictured himself doing" but he had never asked about it. Actually, he admitted, "I was always a little scared of him. He would blow up—not arbitrarily, but usually over something I shouldn't have done."

He and his father connected over one of his father's passions. "He's a math nut. He spends his spare time doing math problems. I was sort of a math nerd myself, so we did that together. I would try to explain my math homework, but of course he was several centuries beyond me."

"When I think of my father," Don summed up wanly, as if speaking from another country, "I think of his enthusiasms, which are separate from his profession: math, track and field, the Brooklyn Dodgers (still)—those things motivate him."

THE SEARCH FOR MODELS

Conrad, Paul, and Don reflect the gamut of father-son intimacies I heard about. Some were truly grim, others well-intentioned but unsatisfying, and a few were companionable in a rather neutral way. None, not one young father I interviewed, spoke of his own father as a role model for the loving, engaged parenting he expected to practice. "It's funny," Conrad commented, "that something so fundamental as fathering is something you should grow up with no conscious exemplar of, no model that you were rebelling against or seeking to emulate or anything. In a vacuum."

Into that vacuum, for the contemporary young father,

flood helpful and not-so-helpful bytes of information, conventional wisdom, off-the-wall wisdom, glimpses of characters from books and movies, as well as the growing expertise of his partner. All that chatter combines with a lifetime of experience with his own parents, other older men, and authority figures. Emotional memories of failure, confusion, and shame are churned up by the doubts and inadequacies parenthood engenders.

It is impossible to identify which perceived mistake is a natural current of the "I'm paddling as fast as I can" business of parenting and which a personal shortcoming, which failure the outcome of bad judgment and which the perversity of circumstances—and, in the end, whether even the most joyous moment owes anything to anyone's parental behavior.

It would help if there were someone with the wisdom of experience to lean on. Some men have found a shadowy grandfather figure—either the one they remember from childhood or the one their own fathers became. Conrad, for example, began to rebuild his own relationship with his father when he saw him, at the end of his life, with his grandchildren. And Paul looks back gratefully on loving contact with his grandfather: "I'm sure he was a terrible father to his sons, but my father's father and I were very close. He lived around the corner from us growing up so I'd see him all the time and he was very warm to me and he made a big effort to see me. So in a way my grandpa Sidney was definitely very accepting of me. And he never criticized me ever. It was just unconditional love."

The phrase "unconditional love" is especially potent to psychologist Elisabeth Kübler-Ross. After watching hundreds of people approach death, she has noticed that more often than anyone would have expected, the dying focus on a relationship with a grandparent that existed perhaps three-quarters of a century before. She suspects that the magnet is the one experience of "unconditional love" in a lifetime. Parents can't give that, she points out; they are too busy with the day-to-day demands of managing a family and disciplining children. Grandparents have the freedom of age—and, perhaps also, the inspiration of regret—to indulge themselves in the luxury of pure love.

It is as though Conrad's and Paul's and other grandfathers I heard about were able to reach across the generations and hug their own sons at last, through the surrogate of grandchildren. Perhaps by being loving grandfathers, they can help guide these transitional fathers—their sons—into a more intimate relationship with their children than they themselves ever knew.

CHAPTER THREE

WORK AND EVERYTHING ELSE
Flying under the Radar

Ted has just gotten some good news: he's been given the ad agency's biggest new account to supervise. His boss puts his arm around Ted's shoulder and to emphasize how much he is counting on Ted tells him, "I'm going to need you one hundred and ten percent—twenty-four hours a day—seven days a week...." Ted is rarin' to go. "I'll give you eight *days a week," he replies.*

When Ted's boss expresses some concern over the fact that Ted has recently become a single father, Ted reassures him.

A few months later, Ted's boss is still nervous. "I'm getting worried," he says when Ted has missed a deadline. "I've got a shop to run," he grumbles, "I can't let your family problems interfere." Once again Ted reassures him.

But finally the accumulated school appointments, medical emergencies, and loss of "face time" in the office add up, and Ted is fired.

Ted manages to get a less-demanding job (for less pay) which is a better fit with his life with his son, Billy, but when his ex-wife sues for custody, her lawyer cites this as a count against his fitness as a father, concluding contemptuously, "You seem to be working your way down the ladder of success."

WHEN THE MOVIE *Kramer vs. Kramer* came out in 1979, its tale of a father's awakening to his nurturing side—and the negative response of almost everyone he tries to deal with—left audiences shaken. They had never seen a movie quite like this and didn't know what to make of the counter-intuitive sympathies the movie generated. Ted, played by Dustin Hoffman, is left with sole responsibility for their six-year-old son, Billy, when his wife, isolated at home and going crazy, leaves him to "find herself." He is forced to fight both the workplace expectations and the legal system's prejudices in order to fulfill what he comes to know is the most important commitment in his life.

Ted was up against an assignment of roles that was as rigid as it was unreflective of reality: Parenting was synonymous with mothering. And a man—a father—was expected, according to Rosabeth Moss Kanter, an observer of corporate America at the time, to "act as though [he] had no other loyalties, no other life" but his work.

Billy would be all grown-up today and perhaps becoming

a father himself, but many of the obstacles that faced Ted still await him. They look a little different, though; joint custody has made some difference, and many of the put-downs of Ted's efforts that seem so heavy-handed to a contemporary viewer of *Kramer vs. Kramer* are now obscured by a professed cultural transformation, all the more insidious for that camouflage.

Despite protestations to the contrary and even some progress in the direction of more flexible and empathic attitudes, most people—men and women—in the workforce have different expectations for a working father than for a working mother. Employers say they are becoming more family friendly, but those in the know pass the word to male coworkers that it is better to call in sick than to take a "family day." Not all working fathers would want or need to adapt their workday to family commitments, but surely they are entitled to the same choices as working mothers, not all of whom opt to take advantage of the benefits available, either. The few men and countless women who do, know all too well that their choice will have some impact on the growth rate of their careers; but while the women can count on respect, if not support, for their decision, men cannot. Moreover, women in the family-work bind are not necessarily men's natural allies; they have their own agendas, including trying to combat persistent salary discrepancies and resentment about lack of support at home.

If the so-called Mommy Track, which in return for concessions to family needs offers a slow track that never seems to connect to the main line, is a mixed blessing, a comparable local timetable for men is a curse. For a man it is still harmful to behave in any way that suggests that work is not far and away the top priority or that he cannot handle any "outside" problems on his own. This need to keep quiet about the rest of his life colludes with male reticence about most things to put the working father into a dark and lonely place that is all the harder to escape from because it is solitary confinement.

There are not many accounts of life behind the wall of silence, where men keep their real priorities. This book tells the stories of men who are trying to bring the rest of their lives into focus along with work. They may not even be the majority of men, or even the majority of fathers, but right now they are not showing up on the screen at all, because anyone who wants to be a father "on company time" quickly learns that he can only do so by flying below the radar.

The good news is that there are more and more of them working and living in a wide range of circumstances. The bad news is that they have no idea of how many like-minded comrades they have.

James Levine, founder of the Fatherhood Project, an unusual organization that tracks the experience of fathers at work, has become an expert in luring them out of the woodwork. Increasingly he is invited to advise employers who feel they need help selling mistrustful employees on their commitment to family concerns. (In fact, some 56 percent of the 1,057 companies evaluated in a 1998 study by the Families and Work Institute report that they do offer "employee assistance programs to help workers deal with problems that may affect their personal lives.") The first thing Levine does when he shows up is to announce a meeting of fathers to discuss common problems; the response is enlightening for both sides. Many of Levine's clients have little sense of how the fathers in their organizations are struggling until a notice goes up inviting them to discuss their work/family conflicts and the session is oversubscribed within hours. The fathers are just as surprised by the turnout. Each thought he was alone.

THE WORKAHOLIC MODEL IS
ALIVE—AND TRAVELING

Granted, the rigid role expectations have broken down. With the influx of mothers into the workplace over the past twenty years, women have taken on other roles than mothering, even if they haven't been able to hand off a comparable share of the demands of parenting and running a household to their partners. It is because of those women that employers have become more sensitive to the needs of working parents, and with the passage of the Family and Medical

Leave Act (which began its laborious trek through the Congress in 1985 and was vetoed by two presidents before Bill Clinton signed it in 1993), employers are now required to be more responsive. But there is still more lip service than real support in America's workplaces, and many of the old attitudes about mixing work and family have only gone below the surface.

I recently heard an energetic young investment analyst enthuse over his electronic workplace; what appeals to him most is that, since the world economy is always open for business, he can now stay plugged in around the clock every day of the year. The way he sees it, never having to leave the office enables him to have it all. "With all the new technology," he announced with satisfaction, "I can now spend more of my weekends with my family!"

He may think that he's freed himself up to balance the two sides of his life, but it isn't hard to imagine the view of him that his family gets on those weekends, plunking away on his laptop and juggling overseas conference calls, or the effort they would have to make to lure him out of range of his mobile office. No matter how generous a family policy his company offers, he can't make use of it, given his work style.

Giant strides in telecommunications, which were once touted as creating more family time and freedom, have made the "24/7" (twenty-four hours a day, seven days a week) mentality a working possibility, generating an array of add-ons to a reasonable workday. Virtually every business is international and many jobs have become "an insatiable maw devouring every waking hour and many sleeping ones too," according to *Fortune* magazine. The worldwide economy has also made business travel one of the most punitive job requirements. The business trip is the most dramatic and quantifiable symbol of work that doesn't work for families.

Showing up several time zones away from home, which used to be a glamorous, if burdensome, duty of high-level executives, has become drudge work for countless salespeople, managers, accountants, and engineers. Despite the technologies of "virtual" contact, or maybe because of them, "face time" has become a more important part of many jobs. With business travel putting more parents on the road every year, many jobs bring this new source of family disruption— and overtime.

To be at a Monday-morning meeting across the country, for instance, a traveling businessman has to leave his home soon after breakfast on Sunday—after having most likely spent most of Saturday back at the office wrapping up loose ends and preparing for the trip. At the other end, the whims of a client may keep the traveler juggling three or four different return tickets and his family unable to finalize plans of their own until they get the word that Dad, albeit groggy with jet lag, is on the way.

For the men describing their struggle to get home from

work, both literally and figuratively, the ability or the courage to renounce travel stands out as the signal act of a truly committed parent.

In some instances the only way out of a travel-intensive career is a change of jobs. That choice is all the more noteworthy when those who fly planes for a living make it. The *New York Times* took note of the growing alarm among Air Force brass at the massive defection of expensively trained pilots who cited the long stretches (some two hundred days a year) away from home as a major reason. In 1996, 498 pilots left; a year later the number was 700, and reenlistment had dropped from 81 percent in 1994 to 30 percent in 1997. "There's been a basic attitude change," explained a thirty-one-year-old F-15E pilot, sounding exactly like his civilian counterparts. "I'll miss the Air Force. I'll miss the camaraderie. When I was 22, flying fighters was all I thought I'd ever want to do. But then after marriage and kids, family becomes more important than a fighter jet. They're your priority."

RALPH SAYS NO

The story of one man's simple request to opt out of just one trip demonstrates how rigid even the least militaristic workplace can be. Ralph, who comes across as a particularly mild-mannered and conscientious employee, works for a major computer publishing company, where dress is casual, employee relations are relaxed, and the policy is family friendly. Nonetheless, the business is international and the travel unrelenting. Last year he was in Ceylon on his daughter Tillie's fourth birthday; she was so disappointed that she extracted a promise from him to be at her fifth birthday party, no matter what. Ralph took his vow so seriously that he even alerted his boss to that inviolate April commitment months ahead. Then, in late winter, something came up—an important management conference. Ralph reminded his boss that he couldn't go. His boss was sympathetic (he has his own young kids) but insistent. "How about if we send your whole family?" he offered. "Wouldn't that be a great birthday present?" Well, not really. Not to a five-year-old who wanted a real birthday party, with favors and friends and cake *and* daddy.

Over the next few weeks, tension between mild-mannered Ralph and his sympathetic boss rose as they tried to resolve the impasse. Ralph was pushing for sending a substitute; his boss was pushing for changing the date of the birthday party.

The story has a happy ending of sorts—Ralph prevailed. A subordinate, whom Ralph briefed during both of their "spare time," went and did a fine job. Ralph attended the birthday party and felt wonderful about having gotten himself there. But the amount of energy and conflict that went into the question of Tillie's birthday party remains a monument to the intransigence of business travel. It also calls to mind the regretful mantra attributed to an anonymous executive at the end of his life: "You will always remember the graduation or birthday you missed, but you will never remember the meeting you missed it for."

SKIN-DEEP SUPPORT

Empathic as he was, Ralph's employer remained captive to a work *über alles* standard he would undoubtedly denounce. (He did offer to fly the whole family to the conference, after all.) It would have been interesting to find out how he would confront the challenge of dealing with an employee he might consider a "real" parent, but that won't happen soon. As Ralph realized as he was telling this story, all the women in the company had opted out of the travel-intensive career track he was on precisely because it was incompatible with family life.

Matt, a thirty-eight-year-old father of twins, doesn't know that he was found wanting against a double standard. His boss, the senior partner in a small law firm, wasn't aware of it himself. Jeff takes pride in having created a "family" among the lawyers that work there; his is one of the very few firms where no one comes in over the weekend or stays late. He tells new attorneys that he only wants to work among people who "have a life," as he puts it. Still Matt was a worry to him; he had begun to feel that the young man simply didn't have "it"; though he worked hard and was smart, something was disappointing about him. Finally, pressed for specific examples, Jeff grumbled, "Well, he just takes off in the afternoons." To do what? "Oh, like his three-year-olds' birthday party. Why couldn't they at least schedule that for five o'clock instead of three o'clock?" He still didn't hear himself until he was asked whether he would resent the same behavior on the part of a woman employee. Then it hit him. Like many employers who are very supportive of working mothers, he had a blind spot about working fathers.

If "good guys" like Matt's boss can feel they are paying their dues by accommodating mothers while holding fathers to a tougher standard more like the one they labored under while raising their own children, it is small wonder that their best intentions are not enough to convince their employees that they really take family commitments seriously. Couples are right to assume that, for example, there would most likely be less fallout from a mother's request to stay home with a family emergency than a father's. That serves to make a self-fulfilling prophecy of the conventional wisdom that it is unseemly for a man to "run home" on family business "in the middle of the day."

Collaborators are everywhere, not just in the workplace, making sure that men stay in their place—at work. I remember once I got back to my desk after a long lunch to find a message from my daughter's school nurse. When I called, I was told that my daughter had come in complaining of a headache and stuffy head around noon and was still there at two-thirty waiting for word about what to do next. I was dismayed that she had languished for so long and demanded to know why my husband hadn't been called. "Oh," the nurse replied blithely, "It wasn't an emergency, and we don't like to bother the daddies."

"Bullshit"—Conrad

Most working men believe that, more often than not, when good intentions come in conflict with business considerations, something has to give, and there are very few reports of it being the business considerations. That was what Conrad discovered when he went into a job with the understanding that, as he told his prospective employer, "I work forty-five hours a week. You will get superlative effort and ability in those forty-five hours a week. You won't regret it for a moment. But that's my deal."

Four years later, he's concluded that "the deal was bullshit in the first place."

At first, as he sees it, "they wanted to hire me, so they said, 'Sure, of course. Of course we're a child-friendly, family-friendly workplace. Nobody works crazy hours here.'" But as the organization grew and prospered, more traditional measures of productivity clicked in. "If somebody is prepared to give you fourteen hours a day for at least as many years that they don't burn out, as opposed to somebody who's going to give you nine hours, you're going to take the fourteen. Anyone is. That's the kind of productivity analysis you make: What is in the best interest of the organization? Is it to be a healthy, harmonious workplace that contributes to our vision of a socially healthy workplace, or is it to kick ass?"

Conrad also noticed another kind of "bullshit"—the fourteen-hour day disguised as nine: "My boss is almost exactly my age, and he has two kids about the same age as mine. He doesn't stay at the office late; he actually leaves at a pretty civilized hour. He makes a great point about leaving at a civilized hour, but when you see him at eight-thirty the next morning, he's got a stack of memos he's written, letters he's drafted, phone calls he's made, to prove that he's working till midnight every single night."

Conrad tries to "do unto others" when hiring subordinates. "The first thing I do is say, 'Do not look at your watch at 5:31 to see if I'm noticing that you're still here. If you need to go home, go home. I want excellence in your work and I want you to do it in a manageable fashion—you don't prove anything to me by staying until nine at night, because I won't be here.' But in terms of stamping that philosophy on the institution as a whole, forget it." Why? "I don't have the force of character to enforce it. I don't believe in the battle enough to fight it for everybody else."

Conrad is a human rights activist. If he isn't ready to take on the system, who is?

The closest that men in Conrad's circumstances get to acknowledging their disappointment is the tried-and-true protective male tradition of sharing war stories. One working father, who is famous among his friends for his efforts to set limits on his workday, has become a lightning rod for grumbling fellow travelers. "The only way I have experienced men talking about all this is telling each other tales about how they told the system no," he says. "This newspaper-reporter friend says, 'I told them fuck you. I don't want to do that. I'm not gonna work ten hours a day. Good-bye'—that's the way he talks. Another friend, who teaches, was asked by the dean to take calls at home from students and be available twenty-four hours a day. The dean said, 'These kids are paying this big tuition, you have to be there for them.' And my friend said, 'No, I won't do it. When I'm home, I'm home.' It's small things like that, but . . . it's individual."

ADVICE TO THE AMBITIOUS

The message that any solution must be individual is reinforced by the voices of professional wisdom. Typical is this advice from a hip on-line adviser, Fast Company: "All you can do," it warns, "is make trade-offs—doing a lot of what you don't like so you can get to the stuff that you really care about. That means, for example, crashing on a deadline until two in the morning, which frees you to spend the weekend with the kids."

When it comes to coping with family responsibilities on work time, the message, Lay low!, is loud and clear. A typical piece of advice comes from the Disney website "Family.com" in a regular column called "Working Solutions" by Susan Crites Price and Tom Price. Under the headline "Beware of the Daddy Track," the column addresses the predicament of a member of the site's on-line community: "My company has generous policies that allow mothers and fathers to miss work to take care of sick children and to avoid travel when possible. Informally, they also allow us to take time off for special events at our children's school. I am one of the few men to take advantage of these policies, and suddenly I'm starting to feel like I'm on the daddy track. I see other men around me getting important accounts, making big presentations and generally moving ahead. Was it a mistake for me to put fatherhood first once in a while?"

The Prices point out, quite rightly, that the questioner's company "sounds more progressive than most" but that such policies won't help "if there is an unspoken view that men who take advantage of the benefits aren't serious about their careers.... If you are one of only a few dads who put a priority on family, you're vulnerable to a boss who equates commitment with hours spent on the job.... Some men with access to the kinds of benefits you describe have decided to move cautiously—using the family-friendly policies judiciously and checking reactions before using them more. If you think your career is threatened, you might want to back off a bit." (On another occasion the Prices were more optimistic, encouraging a man to push for a leave policy for fathers. "By setting an example," they write, "you'll make others feel more comfortable about taking leave.")

"Don't poke your head up above the trenches" is not happy advice, but it is realistic. The military metaphor is reinforced by a scan of the men in any rush-hour crowd. The vast majority are disguised in the standard-issue suit and tie— the Conrads and Ralphs along with everyone else. Psychologist Harriet Lerner sees a grim message in the picture: "I think the colorlessness, the rigidity of style, and the tie knotted around the neck all serve to blunt men's emotional responsiveness and prepare them for a military mentality." Women's attire, on the other hand, reflects the extent to which they have broken the mold. Having survived the dress-for-success uniform, they are much more relaxed and expressive in their work clothes. And much freer to move around the culture in whatever they think looks and feels best. Thanks to years of protests and boycotts (eternal verities die hard), there are clubs and restaurants that admit women in all manner of short skirts and long pants, but the same establishments keep an assortment of ties and jackets on hand to make sure the men conform.

Lerner wonders what would happen if, as a "cultural experiment," men and women "totally switched 'dress codes' for one year." The sight of men dressed in more revealing or more casual clothing would, she is certain, "freak most people out." That, in truth, is what happens in many workplaces when men try to assume the metaphorical baggy, pastel, and broken-in accoutrements of parenthood at the office.

"It's fine to have the kids' pictures on your desk—just don't let them cut into your billable hours," warns a 1997 article entitled "Is Your Family Wrecking Your Career? (And Vice Versa)" in *Fortune* magazine, the bible of corporate America. The "dirty little secret" exposed in the article is that while companies pay "more lip service than ever" to families and even put their policies where their mouths are, "corporate manuals would do well to carry a warning: Ambitious beware. If you want to have children, proceed at your own risk. You must be very talented, or on very solid ground, to overcome the damage a family can do to your career."

And, as the headline warns, vice versa.

A WAKE-UP CALL—BRIAN

By the time Brian, who is now thirty-six, graduated college, he was married and a father; two years later, he set out on an exciting career in finance. He was caught up in his work and also very aware of the need to provide for his growing family. As far as he had ever known, this was the right thing. When his son and daughter were little, he was working long weekdays and weekends. "And when I wasn't working, I was taking naps on the couch," he adds, his open face clouding over at the recollection. "I was overwhelmed and overworked." That went on for ten years. The wake-up call came in the form of a summons from the guidance counselor at his son's school, who had also been the guidance counselor when Brian himself went to that same suburban school. "I went in and he said, 'I'm really fond of you. I'm really fond of your son; he is a great kid and he has good values but he's starting to drift off the beaten path.' I had noticed there was a fair amount of tension beginning between the two of us," Brian recalls ruefully, "but I had just chalked it up to twelve-year-old boys rebelling against their fathers." But the guidance counselor laid it on the line: "Your son is starting to hang out with kids who are having behavioral problems," he told Brian. "You need to encourage him to get back with the other kids in his peer group. However you do it, you need to do that."

"I was kind of shocked," Brian admits. "I said, 'What can I do?' He gave me the best piece of fatherly advice I've ever gotten in my life: 'Spend time with your son.' I thought about it and I said, 'I'm around a lot.' And he said, 'No—

spend time with your son. And make him understand that you're spending time with *him*—whatever it is—if you're home, make him know that you're there with him or make priority things—take him to a ball game, whatever—spend time with your son.'"

Brian knew he had to change his work life in order to follow that advice. It wasn't easy to find a more forgiving work situation; he tried teaching for a while and then ended up at a very low-key financial operation run by an old and understanding friend. "I really made the decision to put my career on hold for four or five years and spend time—quality *and* quantity time—with the kids and really enjoy them. If you spend a lot of time with your kids, instead of just popping up and being the bad guy, there's good times and bad times to share. You talk about sports, you talk about grades, about whatever, and then when you want to make a point it's almost like you're entitled to make a point. As opposed to showing up on the weekends or at seven-thirty at night and making your point then; and the only thing sticking in his mind is the dad being home making a point."

Brian's relationship with his son didn't improve overnight. It took great patience on Brian's part and a humility that I found poignant. "Billy had a lot of resentment and anger that I had ignored him," he explains. "I was surprised at how much I had not paid attention to him for all those years; he was a low priority. He was angry about that and he took it out on me, but after those words of advice, I just took it. Just let him vent. I didn't get mad, didn't tell him 'You can't talk to me that way.' He finally got all that anger out of his system. It took time."

Among other things, Brian's decision to get off the fast track forced the family to make financial sacrifices, such as staying in a small crowded apartment in the suburban community where they live, while all the other families they knew were buying their own homes. But Brian has come to see his dream of having it all in sequential terms. "I was young enough at the time to say I'm not going to make Wall Street money, but I'm not going to have Wall Street hours or expectations or pressures. I'll spend five years with the kids and that's where I'm going to get some reward. At the end of that, I'll be thirty-eight or -nine and then I can pursue career number two." He envies those men he knows who have been able to do it the other way around. "At some point you get your career under control and it's manageable. The majority of parents we know are older and they had their kids when they were thirty and had a better ability to balance work and family. I'd say in the nineties, your twenties are for your career and your thirties and forties are to blend family and career."

The way Brian sees it, men can have it all if they don't make the same mistakes he did. But the holy grail of perfect balance was just as out of reach for those who have taken other routes. All found the choices limited and the measures of success more modest.

THE INVISIBLE MAN

The combination of mistrust and mixed messages surrounding family and work issues for men helps explain why, despite the upswing in working alternatives that include job sharing, and modified numbers of hours on the job, men are infinitely less likely than women to avail themselves of these choices. Instead, they look for other ways of doing what they hope will enable them to have their cake and eat it too, to be both daddy and paterfamilias at the same time.

So, when men do take steps to preserve family time, they don't do it in a way that accumulates statistics about non-work commitments; as a result, the message of their choice is muted. It has been widely noted, for example, that men do not take formal parental leave, despite the fact that a substantial minority are eligible and in some cases the leave is paid. But that is not the whole story, according to University of Illinois psychologist Joseph H. Pleck, an authority on masculinity. When he hears from a manager that no one has taken leave, Pleck probes further. What happened, he asks, the last time a man who works there had a child? The answer proves not how reluctant men are to take time for their young children, but how careful they are to protect their image. Manager after manager told Pleck of new fathers who took a combination of "vacation days, sick days, compensatory time off, and other informal time."

In other words, men beat the system, Pleck concludes, by using family policies selectively "to the extent that their use (*a*) does not reduce their earnings, weakening their role and identity as breadwinners, and (*b*) does not cause them to be perceived as uncommitted to their jobs or unmasculine."

Now You See Him; Now You Don't—Carl

Carl is a particularly intriguing example of someone who knows how to play the duck-and-feint game. Appropriately, he is a former basketball star, who went on to become an executive with a professional sports team and is now a human resources manager at a large firm. He sees the family pressures both professionally and—since seven months before we talked—personally. When his son, Raymond, was born, his priorities shifted "at a gut level." He had been, in his words, "one of the most ambitious people you could meet" but then, all of a sudden "where work had been really important, money had been really important, getting out and having a good time had been really important, all of those things hit the back burner very, very quickly." His priority is now getting home to be with his son. "If that means I'm not going to get as high up the chain as I would have, so be it. So I won't be a corporate maven; I'm OK with that."

But does he take advantage of the family-friendly programs that it is his job to offer other employees? Not really. Nor do the men he counsels. "I don't see that men who take advantage of the work-at-home program do it for child-care reasons, for example, but I think in the back of their minds it's to be at home with the kids. Many of the women say they work at home to be around the kids or to alleviate child-care costs; I've yet to hear a man say 'I want to work from home because I want to be able to take care of the kids.'"

Carl has been able to tailor his schedule without appearing to. His work requires him to travel among his organization's outlying branches, so he has some flexibility—and some invisibility. "I know Monday I'm at one site, Tuesday I'm at another, and so on through the week. I have certain rules for my calendar. My admin does my calendar and she knows that on Friday I am at a particular site because it's five minutes from my home, so my wife and I can meet for lunch and I'm close to home at the end of the week. I have told her to do all she can to avoid scheduling meetings after three o'clock. That way there is less chance that something will come up—a meeting that runs over—that will cause me to be late for what I call my second job," his six o'clock commitment to his son.

Carl had to attain a certain amount of status to be able to design this schedule and even so, he admits, "There are certain things that I feel somewhat uncomfortable about having to bring up, and I definitely look over my shoulder as I'm walking out the door at five or five-thirty. Because everyone else is still actively working."

Well, not exactly everyone. It only looks that way to the guilty few. "There are some people that I see that are in very similar situations to me," Carl concedes. "We know who we are. We're like a support group, you know like AA; you never really identify who you are or what you are, but you all know who each other are. It's going to take a lot to change, because there are societal as well as corporate pressures."

If Carl, the human resources manager, won't take advantage of family-friendly policies, who will?

WALKING OFF THE JOB ... EVERY DAY—NICK

Nick has created his own family-friendly work history without benefit of policy or subterfuge. A no-frills, earnest kind of guy, he didn't set out to be a pioneer but understands that his outspoken defense of his island of domesticity has made him one. A little shy and very respectful, a style that recalls his formal Catholic upbringing, he becomes animated and downright fiery on the subject of holding out for balance. He never got on the fast track that Brian had to jump off, but whereas Brian may have walked out on the career he was building, Nick, now in his forties, literally walks off the job every single day.

He is regularly reminded of how iconoclastic his commitment is. "I had an interesting argument with a friend of mine who was bitching about what he sees as a new class of women at work who he calls 'prima donnas.' He says they expect to get ahead and yet they expect to not do their share. I said, 'I have walked out in midmeeting, midsentence, and it's not because I'm a prima donna, it's because I have a priority. And the system ought to be able to deal with that. I do make up for it in other ways. I'm incredibly efficient.' Then we talked about what his day is like. He sits around and bullshits and spends half an hour complaining about these women—while they're working!"

Nick doesn't deny that he envies his friend's ability to indulge "the schmooze factor." It's "not only relaxing, but useful and helps your creativity and so forth. But something's gotta go. You just have to be ultraefficient," he explains. "I never stop. I eat at my desk—I do my e-mail and stuff like that while I'm eating lunch. You go in. You sit down. You work." And when you have squeezed the maximum amount of work into the given time frame, you leave. "It doesn't make the boss happy to see you walk out," Nick acknowledges, "but you gotta do what you gotta do. I made a choice, I will be home, that's my first priority, and if others don't like it, I'm sorry. It's not like 'fuck you,' but it's like 'I gotta go, so long.'

"People have children and they need to know them, and they need to take care of them," says Nick the evangelist. "It's just something that shouldn't be treated like an emergency; I see a lot of people who don't know their kids and I think it's lousy. It's not that we go home and talk about Shakespeare or our deepest needs, it's usually 'I want a sandwich' and all that, but that matters. And I made a commitment to be there as much as I could. It's just not being a prima donna, it's being a parent."

WITHOUT WORK, WHAT IS HE?

It's not surprising that Nick empathizes with women on the so-called Mommy Track. "I understand," he says about his kind of career, "that you can't be the *top*. At least for a time, you can't be the top." His blend of family and work commitments is more typical of theirs. It puts him on their side of what Joseph Pleck calls the "asymmetrically permeable" boundary that allows family "to intrude upon women's work, whereas for men, work intrudes upon family." The burden falls on working mothers to devise strategies that will enable them to juggle their responsibilities, while men must devise strategies to take on only as much family responsibility as the workplace allows. In their book, *She Works/He Works*, Rosalind Barnett and Caryl Rivers point out a common assumption: "Women need a mommy track," the logic goes, but—

thanks in part to the Mommy Track—"daddies can do it all." In other words, men can have it all—if by "all" they don't mean *all*.

DADDY'S HOME!—ROBERT

A major assumption of the Mommy Track is that there will be points in a woman's career when she may want to be a full-time parent; there is no such assumption about the course of a man's work life. It is almost inconceivable that a man would find satisfaction outside of work. It is almost as unnatural to imagine a man with an identity separate from what he does for a living. That is the heart of the problem.

Robert, a forty-two-year-old father of two young daughters, had the opportunity to look the culture in the eye. Because of a generous severance package from his last job and because his wife brings home a solid paycheck, he was able to stay home with their children for almost a year beginning when they were four months and three years old. He found total immersion in parenting a joyous surprise, but he found being a male in the parenting community a very different kind of surprise.

The first thing he noticed was that there was no "infrastructure" for men outside of work and that his presence even caused some discomfort. That made him wonder how much of the talk about a new kind of fatherhood was genuine. "Even if they think, 'Gee, that's something I would like to do someday,' the fact is that people try to figure out why he is staying home. Is it because he can't find work? Is he staying home because he's failed in his work life somehow and this is just what he's fallen into?" He felt victim of a clear double standard: "Women have more choices. A woman who decides to work and not stay home is not considered to be abandoning her kids anymore. And for women who stay home for a while, there are a lot of societal rewards. People understand that and they think it is great." The women he is talking about would protest that they pay a huge price in terms of worry, exhaustion, and personal time, but, Robert would argue, at least they get sympathy. Men like himself, on the other hand, "just don't feel that society supports their staying home with kids or that other men support that or that work supports that."

The second thing he noticed is that men are unlikely to work to dismantle misperceptions about themselves to the extent that women have worked to change society's attitudes. Women "tend to be much more willing to fight for the ability to balance work and home life than men are," Robert found. "I don't think that men think it's manly to form together and push for more rights to be with their kids. Men are a lot more isolating; they're not 'Let's get together' kinds of guys." By way of illustration he recounts a personal anecdote. "I go to a program with my daughter on Saturday mornings for dads and kids. It's like an hour of play and art projects. But there's absolutely no communication between me and the other dads there. If it were a group for moms and kids, after one or two sessions there would be three or four women who would be saying, 'Why don't we get together?'"

Finally, he zeroes in on the ambivalence that holds so many fathers back. "We have a friend in Sweden and he's just decided to take basically the rest of the year off. Their society is much more geared towards equality and towards very long, extended parental leaves without any negative consequences. In ours, it's not geared that way. Sure, there is a lot more job sharing at work, maternity leaves, parental leaves. But I don't think that a lot of guys would take advantage of that kind of thing, because it's still a little bit odd to a lot of people. It's just not the usual."

COMING OUT FROM BEHIND
THE IRON MASK

The fiction that real men don't need help keeps real fathers hidden behind cardboard fronts or behind mother-friendly offerings. No wonder then, that the message isn't getting out. Although nearly half the workforce is composed of dual career couples, "employers know very little about how these couples function and what they want or need in the workplace," according to findings by Catalyst, the research and advisory organization that has been monitoring gender issues in the workplace for fifteen years.

Employers also have been slow to factor in the costs of their ignorance. They are just waking up to the business consequences of running an inhospitable workplace. One executive woke up because a personal tragedy forced him to confront family-work conflicts by living them. When his wife, who had handled the household and child rearing, died of cancer in 1981, Hewlett-Packard's Lewis E. Platt was left to raise his two daughters, ages nine and eleven, while at the same time maintaining his hard-driving career. "I was suddenly thrust into a different role," he recalls. The experience shattered his old assumption that the difficulties women executives were having were of their own making. "I couldn't cope any better than they did," he admits.

Platt went on to become the company's CEO and made it his mission to reflect what he had learned firsthand about family demands in corporate policy. Hewlett-Packard now offers flexible work schedules, work-at-home options, shared jobs, and unpaid sabbaticals. By doing good for his employees, Platt did well for his company. The turnover rate there is less than a third of the industry average of 17 percent. "Anything you can do to attract and retain the best talent is really critical," he points out.

The same conclusion has been reached at Federal Express, where the 9 percent attrition rate became such a concern that the company is experimenting with offering on-site day care to employees. Recruitment Manager David Huffer told *Business Week* magazine that he has seen a 10 percent improvement in employee retention where it was available. He estimates that to replace one of their 40,000 operations employees costs about a half year's pay.

It is also costly to cover absences due to parental responsibilities. Employers are beginning to take seriously such dollars and cents findings as those released by Work-Family Directions of Boston, a company that advises companies on work and family policy, that 70 percent of working parents missed at least one day in the previous year because of child-related problems, and that according to the Child Care Action Campaign, a national advocacy group, such absences cost U.S. businesses an estimated $3 billion a year.

Little by little, employers are also being forced to recognize the needs of the invisible parent, the working father. According to Ellen Galinsky of the Families and Work Institute, an organization that explores workplace issues and often conducts focus groups, "When we first started doing this, the groups of men and of women sounded very different. If the men complained at all about long hours, they complained about their wives' complaints. Now if the timbre of the voice was disguised, I couldn't tell which is which. The men are saying: 'I don't want to live this way. I want to be with my kids.' I think the corporate culture will have to begin to respond to that." But first, in order for attitudes to catch up with experience, the voices in Galinsky's focus groups need to go public.

Where are the men who are willing to stand up for family the way their forefathers stood up for country? They are there, and they will find each other—if not in protest marches, then in the quick-getaway corners of workplace parking lots. As they stand up, they will be counted. And leaders will emerge—if not because they have the courage to speak out, then because they have the power to change the rules.

CHAPTER FOUR

TRADE-OFFS

Buying Time to Parent

*There may be only two kinds of consumers in the world:
those who have children and those who don't.... Parents
with children under the age of 18 are unique because
their money and their time are controlled by their children's wants and needs. They are hard to reach with advertising messages because their attention is not focused
on themselves.... If the big spenders of the 1980s seem to
be disappearing, it's only because of a massive shift in
their priorities.*

    —Cheryl Russell, "On the Baby-Boom Bandwagon,"
American Demographics, May 1991

THE "MASSIVE SHIFT IN PRIORITIES" that has moved huge
blocks of spending from self to children has also created a
growing population of men in the predominantly female
ranks of those trying to balance work and family. And one
thing is becoming clear to them, as it did to the wised-up and

burned-out women of the last decade: you cannot have it all. The simple fact is the "all" doesn't fit into real time, at least as constituted on this planet. Working fathers are discovering that even piecing together some of it all requires them to invest all they have in the business of balancing, juggling, and buying time.

Time for what? To get the job done, to get the other jobs done, to meet unending commitments, to fulfill relentless responsibilities, but most of all to *be there* for their kids. To be there as their kids happen.

Nick, father of three, puts it this way: "Problems that kids are having or thoughts that they're having—they don't come out on schedule. If you're not there, you don't know anything. Or those moments that make a bond. They come out by being there, you being in the right place."

Bill walks his seven-year-old daughter to school every day. "It's a nice time to share," he says. "To be relaxed. I just think holding hands with a child walking down the street is really special." For him "being immersed" in his children's lives has been the "biggest change" in his own life. If he hadn't made the time to be there, he would not have come to understand what now seems to him a "miracle." "I used to think that growing up was evolutionary. You expect gradual changes as they pick up skills. But it happens overnight. My older daughter didn't walk for the first sixteen months; then we were at a family funeral for my great aunt, and the whole family was around, and from one minute to the next she was walking. We were all wrapped up in the emotions of loss, and suddenly there she was!"

To Nick and Bill and the thousands like them, it is a self-evident truth that when it comes to children, "quantity time is a prerequisite to quality time," which is how Ken. R. Canfield has put it in his book *The Heart of a Father.* "It takes quantity time," Canfield insists, "to build a relationship of mutual trust, and trust is absolutely necessary for real quality time."

THE TRADING GAME

With two hard jobs to do, and only twenty-four hours to do them in, working parents will do just about anything to get a little control of their time. When asked what they look for in a job by pollsters, 85 percent responded "flexible hours." For an offer of those precious hours, parents willingly trade salary, benefits, workday schedules, and advancement. But that is rarely enough. They must also look to their personal treasury for goods—private time, outside interests or training, and sleep—to barter for the chance to make child rearing a priority. If they have made themselves demographically invisible as consumers, it is because they have virtually traded themselves away.

Robert, who has succeeded (on a good day) in creating a

time zone for children in his life by scaling back on hours at work and on the kind of work he does and by spending much less time with friends, sees the stakes in terms of "an equation. It's really hard to find that equilibrium between home and social life and work," what he and his friends call "the Triple Crown." "You are always trying to have great experiences in all three of those at the same time," he says. "Somehow, when one or two are doing really well, the other one is not going well and it's really hard to achieve that high level of satisfaction in all three of those. It just depends on what you're willing to sacrifice for what."

Bill, who loves his job—he is responsible for worker safety in a pharmaceutical manufacturing company—feels that he has not lost career momentum, but he has passed up the fun and stimulation of spending more time at his work and, surprisingly, on work-related travel. "I go to manufacturing sites and try to help employees manage certain issues of chemical exposure, ergonomics, machine safety. I talk to people, try to come up with alternative designs, evaluate chemical processes. It's very interesting. And I always learn something." But learning has to be reined in if he is going to maintain balance. He tried to explain that at a departmental meeting recently. "The subject of 'professional development' came up. It's great that the company offers people the chance to take courses and seminars. But, I told them, I see it as dessert. And I want everyone to know that if people like me don't take advantage of dessert, it's not because we don't appreciate the dessert, or because we are not hungry, but because we are trying to eat well-balanced meals."

TRADING FOR WHAT?

When the trade-off is clear—if I leave the office at five, I'll have two hours to be with the kids—it is easier to keep an eye on the light at the end of the tunnel, but it can be demoralizing to discover that more of the hard-won minutes and hours end up going to horrid little details and picking up the pieces of unravelled plans. The experience of fathers who have taken on the "second job" of family life may look a lot like that of women who took on a second (paid) job a generation earlier, but there is one big difference: a woman's second job was in many ways more orderly and controllable than the one at home—she had more to show for her time; for men the opposite is true. When a man commits himself to greater participation in home life, with its unpredictability and thankless tasks, he is taking on a second job that brings with it a higher degree of frustration and lower level of status than the one he is paid for. This downside to the glory of parenthood generally comes as a big shock.

Andrew, one of the fathers who has thrown himself into both jobs, sees the difference between them. "I read an article about how women were escaping to the workplace because they didn't want to be home with the kids. It's been like that for men for years and years, and suddenly it's like that for women, too. I can see why. Work is a totally controlled environment—there aren't so many variables. Look at the variables that you're dealing with when you talk about a nineteen-month-old child. It's nothing but variables. You don't know what's going to be happening. When I take a week off like I did last week with the boys, just me and the boys, I love it. But it's hard work."

Robert, who spent a long stretch as the stay-at-home parent, admits that for many people it must seem easier to be at work. "For a lot of people, it would be really nice—in theory—to be home more, but in reality that is very, very, very hard to do."

TIME IS OF THE ESSENCE

Compromise and chaos can seem like the more workable parts of a life thrown off kilter by the ticking of the clock: Serendipity, once a delight, is experienced as crisis; and completing tasks, once an annoying drudgery, becomes a life goal. Lost are the opportunities to let a three-year-old stomp in the mud on the way home from the supermarket, to take a coffee break with coworkers and pick up on shifting sands within the organization, to follow through then and there on the inkling that a teenager is worried about something, to finish reading that book or article, to finish anything.

And very specifically and practically, all kinds of domestic standards—about cleaning, cooking, even economizing—fall by the wayside in such daily triage as: clean house, clean kids, or (your own) clean hair?

Not to mention privacy, leisure—and sex.

Even the children, for whom the race is being run, are not exempt from the tyranny of time. As parents squeeze hours mercilessly from their sleep and pass like ships in the night en route to child-care duty, their kids are forced to live with the vagaries of even the best-laid plans. Unpredictable and fragmented schedules that reflect complex child-care arrangements create a junior version of the time bind—a pervasive sense of always having to "hurry up and wait."

Parents assume that their kids resent the jobs that are their rivals for mom and dad's time, and the guilt about "not being there" compounds their anxiety, but that is not quite the case. According to thousands of interviews done by Ellen Galinsky for her fascinating book *Ask the Children: What America's Children Really Think about Working Parents*, kids have no problem with their parents working and they don't blame lack of time for what bugs them, which is stressed-out behavior at home. They complain of their parents' short tempers and distracted attention in much the same way that adults complain about teenagers. One youngster told Galinsky that when he suspects that his parents are not listening, he throws a nonsense phrase—"Goldfish on the grass"—into the middle of a sentence to see if they notice.

For parents, the stress is one more symptom of the time bind. In surveys, they lament that "time pressures on working families" are getting worse (64 percent) not better (17 percent) and that "finding time for both work and family responsibilities" has gotten harder (59 percent), not easier (22 percent) for families like theirs over the past five years.

The perception that along with more responsibilities we have less time is not wrong. What with work expanding to fill the electronic universe and stripped-down payrolls creating the need for more overtime from the bare-bones staff, Harvard economist Juliet Schor has calculated that the average employed person is now on the job an additional 163 hours per year compared to 1969—the equivalent of an extra month of work! (Almost half of all working parents report working more than forty hours a week.) And when disposable time goes down, the seams give way. Absence due to stress has gone up threefold since 1995. But as of 1997, the major reason for time *lost* from work is no longer illness, but family-related demands (including elderly parents, who are a significant and increasing preoccupation of this "sandwich generation").

It is hard to imagine a work life more unrelenting than that of medieval serfs, but, according to Schor, benighted as they were, they had it better than contemporary families. Although their typical working day stretched from dawn to dusk, there were halts "for breakfast, lunch, the customary afternoon nap, and dinner." In addition "the medieval calendar was filled with holidays. Official—that is, church—holidays included not only long 'vacations' at Christmas, Easter, and midsummer but also numerous saints' and rest days.... All told, holiday leisure time in medieval England took up probably one-third of the year."

Our holidays, days off, and weekend are devoted to errands and catch-up, not leisure, companionship, and reflection. As one minister, who was bemoaning the decline of church attendance, commented in *Fortune* magazine, "Even Jesus had to pull away from his preaching and performing of miracles to rest and relax, to have some private time and prayer."

If working parents had the time to pray, they would undoubtedly pray for time.

BALANCING THE EQUATION—SORT OF

Most of the men I met were scrambling to make deals with the system and with their partners in an effort to squeeze it all in, with limited success. Certain supporters like a reliable child-care center or household help make an enormous difference. But for the most part what holds the high wire up for the more successful balancing acts is unusual flexibility in the work schedule of at least one parent. Those who felt pretty good about the win-lose ratio would say that they and their wives have made it work—sort of.

"Free-floatingness"—Don

"There's a kind of seamlessness to my life," Don told me, evoking an image that all the others would envy. "It's not 'My job is my job, and when I go there, I'm working, and when I'm home, I'm something else.' It's more kind of 'This is what I am.'" He attributes his good fortune to "time flexibility," which, he is aware, most people "in regular office jobs"— including his wife, Beverly, who works in publishing—don't have. He teaches at a major urban university that offers a generous family-leave policy and supports an excellent day-care facility. His home is a short walk across the campus.

When their son, Sam, was born in June, Beverly took leave from her publishing job and stayed home for three months; then in September Don began his semester of leave and took over, with the help of a part-time baby-sitter. Now Sam, who is almost three, is in morning day care, and Don is back at work, but he is still actively involved in Sam's day. "Being in academia made it easier," he admits. "I don't have to be in my office at any particular time. My fixed time obligations are very limited. I have to teach; I have to have office hours; I have to go to meetings. But that probably doesn't take up more than ten hours a week. If I need to go pick Sam up or take him to the doctor, no one looks at me funny. It's not that I work less, but I go home and work. The free-floatingness is one of the things I like about it."

He has given up very little: some hobbies he was rather fond of and going out, but not his subscription to the opera. "Bev and I and another friend of ours have two subscriptions for the three of us, and we kind of switch off," he explains. Also, those things don't seem as important now. He admits that he was "terrified about having kids" because he would have to give up the freedom of going out on the spur of the moment, but it hasn't been so bad, partly because the evenings are an element in the trade-off for time. "We're more likely to spend evenings at home working, both of us."

BUYING TIME WITH DOLLARS—ALAN

Alan's trade-off had an actual price tag; he paid it partly because he saw how much his own father had missed being around his children.

"My father drove a truck for a baking company," he remembers. "And he had the kind of job where he'd work six days a week; he left at five in the morning and didn't get home until six at night. When he was home, he would spend time with us, but he was tired. It's funny, he won't say it around my mother, but when he comes over and he's alone, he tells me how sorry he was that he couldn't spend more time with us when we were young. One of the decisions that I made earlier on in my career was not to be away from home so much."

When Alan married Catherine, who is a nurse, he was headed toward an academic career; then he was recruited by a market research company in the private sector. He quickly found he liked the work, it paid well, and he was good at it. "Over the three years I worked there, I had gotten a number of raises and was doing very well in the company," he says. "Then Bobby was born, and I realized that I was spending way too much time working." From that vantage point, the academic track began to look awfully good again, so he left the marketing job. "The half of my friends that worked with me at the company thought I was nuts, and the management of the company thought I was nuts and tried to convince me that I was making the wrong decision. Of course, those on the academic side where I was coming back thought it was an 'enormously important decision' filled with 'lots of integrity,'" he adds, laughing. It cost him $20,000 in income.

"In retrospect, I'm happy that I made the decision," he goes on. "I am still doing work—teaching and consulting—that I love, and I earn enough money, but back when I made it, it was a major financial sacrifice. I was kind of enjoying the professional career and the success I was having at the company. I began to not enjoy the larger amount of traveling and the number of hours a week I was working after I had an infant at home."

BUYING TIME BY DEGREES—ROBERT

Robert sounds the same note when he describes his decision to downshift his work life. "Especially when you have a newborn, if you're away for a week, that's a pretty large percentage of their life and you miss a lot." At the time he was "in a job where, on certain weeks I was going in to work at four in the morning and I was getting home at eight or eight-thirty or nine at night. It really was ninety to a hundred hours, including going in Sunday afternoons, and that became hard when we had the baby."

He has spent the four years since then trying to ratchet down his professional life—as a television producer—to a schedule which permits both breakfast and dinner at home. He has moved from one job to another, and at one point he spent almost a year out of the workforce altogether at home caring for his two daughters. When he went back to work, he was determined to "get the best of both worlds for a little longer."

His quest for "manageable work hours, not necessarily nine to five, but predictable" has led Robert most recently to take on a six-month project "with zero pressure." What is he willing to trade for that predictability? "I've just gotten to the point where I'm willing not to be as ambitious about moving up the ladder as I was, in exchange for being able to make a good living, have an interesting job, and still be home." At forty-two, he doesn't expect his career "to rise that much more. I'm not willing to make the sacrifices that are necessary for that. I don't think that's my personality right now. I'm just not a type A personality enough to do that kind of work. But," he reminds himself, "there's a level below that, that you can be pretty comfortable at. If you have kids, if that becomes important enough to you, then that can make up for not advancing your career as much, as long as you feel that you're supporting your family, you're doing something interesting, and you're also doing well by your kids. Then I think that whole equation together can work."

But having been home full-time, he understands that a time bind is unavoidable for working parents. "When you go back to work, the time that you have at home becomes much more densely packed. When we come home, there's really no downtime; you don't want the downtime, you want to spend it with the kids, but you always feel like you're sort of in a rush to get everything done. You want to eat and you want to have a little bit of time to relax, so you always feel like you're on a sort of fast downhill slide. What I also find difficult is with our four-year-old daughter, that it's late in the day for her and she's tired. You walk in and you want to spend some good time with her, but she's not always prepared to. It would be a lot better to have those two hours be from four to six instead of six to eight."

Running in Place But Getting Where
He Set Out For—Nick

Nick and Martha, who have been married twenty years and have three children, ages ten, twelve, and sixteen, restricted their career ambitions to a series of unconventional arrangements, made possible by the fact that they did the same kind of work. Soon after they got married, they persuaded the copy chief at a magazine that they could share one copyediting job; it was up to them which one would show up on a given day, but they guaranteed their estimable boss that the job would get done. Later they talked their way into a shared editing job. The idea was that with each at home part of the time, they would both be able to pursue their first love, magazine writing, which would also supplement their income, and when the children they hoped to have came along, one of them would always be home.

It didn't quite work out that way. "I think initially we thought we'd just put the kids in a drawer and work all day," Mike admits with a chuckle. "They turned out to be a little more time-consuming than that." As a result, the freelancing didn't pan out at the level they had hoped and the expenses began to build. By the time their third child came along, one salary was not enough. Nick took over the job they had shared, commuting forty-five minutes each way, but he remained committed to being at home (awake) for at least as many hours as he was at work. Martha took a position at the local newspaper, passing up offers of higher-level jobs farther away. Nick enjoys what he does, but he has not moved up the masthead, and he has done almost no freelance writing. That, as he sees it, is the deal. "I just didn't want work to be my only focus. I think that took something off. But I'm not unhappy. I'd rather be part of a happy family than have a big byline. I'm satisfied with what I do and where I am and what I know. And I like the time I get to have with my children."

"I guess I was motivated in part by just not doing what was done to me," he adds, sounding a familiar refrain. "My father worked endless hours, and it's no good. It's damaging. You can't really be a parent if you're not there."

Being there for his children meant very specifically being there when they got home from school. That was a promise Nick and Martha made to themselves when they started their family, that they would make things work without babysitters. Meeting that commitment involved some pretty fancy footwork.

"At the beginning, I worked days and she had a night copyediting job, midnight to 6:00 A.M.," recalls Nick weakly, as though still worn-out from the experience. "It's hard to remember how we did things, but I think she slept while the kids were at school. I got them to school, and she would wake up in time to go get them. Then she'd have the whole after-school thing. As soon as I got home, I'd take over so she could rest and get ready, and she'd go. That worked about a year or so until she finally got an offer to go days."

At first, "days" meant getting to work at 6:00 A.M. "So we did the same thing. I would take the kids in the morning and she would pick them up after school when she got off work." Finally a couple of years ago, Martha went on a more regular schedule, 10:00 to 6:00, which coordinates with the 8:30 to 3:30 schedule Nick has managed to extract from his boss (in exchange for working through lunch), but only because she works in the community where they live and can take what is laughably called her "lunch hour" late, at 2:30. "She gets them all home," Nick explains, "gives them a snack, says hello, goes back to work. And then I'm home shortly thereafter with the groceries to start dinner and to get the homework going. Emily is sixteen now, so she can watch the little ones for a couple of hours. Which makes things a bit easier. It used to be terrible if I was three seconds late for the bus, because if I missed one bus, it was thirty minutes till the next one came."

TRADING DAY AND NIGHT: THE TWO-SHIFT SOLUTION

A growing number of couples buy time by creating a formal version of the jigsaw puzzle of shifts that Nick and Martha have adapted to their needs. Shift workers include emergency-room technicians and truck drivers, factory workers and fire-fighters, custodial employees and pilots. They are enough of a population to have their own newsletter (*Working Nights*) which offers advice on sleep (!), health, and marriage (the divorce rate is double that of those with regular hours due to stress at home and temptations from a "nighttime community less committed to conventional lifestyles"). The organization that publishes the newsletter, Circadian Information, also offers a special calendar to help families keep track of one another—it comes with stick-on labels to identify the shift du jour: "night," "evening," "12-hour," "day," "on call," and "relief," as well as "payday," "vacation," and "off." That array of variables offers a hint of how complicated this trade-off can be.

In 1993, 1.3 million of all the employed fathers with children under age five—about 23 percent—took care of their children while their wives were at their jobs. (At the same time, they also did more housework than their nine-to-five counterparts, according to *Working Nights.*) For most it is a job and they are making the best of it, but for some it is a choice; they have found that punching a time clock at odd hours gives them access to important parts of the day.

Christopher, father of a six-year-old and a newborn, leaves before dawn for his shift as a power-line worker and gets home at 4:30, when his wife is getting ready to leave for her 6:00 P.M. to 2:30 A.M. job as a dispatcher. He is very happy with the setup. "I like coming home to take care of the kids," he told a *New York Times* reporter in 1998. "I feel I can talk to my son. He's closer to me than I was to my parents. I can come home every single night and be with him." A downside to the trade-off they have made is that he cannot say the same about his relationship with his wife.

Indeed, "what may be good for the children may not be good for the marriage," says Dr. Harriet Presser, a professor at the University of Maryland who is an authority on shift work. Occasionally, though, the partnership can be a revelation. Stephanie, who works the 6:30 A.M. to 2:00 P.M. shift for a clothing manufacturer in Seattle, told Sue Shellenbarger, work-and-family columnist for the *Wall Street Journal,* that she "fell in love all over again" with her husband, Mike, who works at a photo shop from 3:00 to 10:00 P.M., when she saw how wonderful he was with the kids. That feeling compensates for the fact that in order to be with their kids, they don't see each other—awake—during the week, except at "hand-off" time.

Jonathan, who was also interviewed by the *Times,* scaled back his career trajectory after he realized he was spending up to seventy hours a week away from his family. He quit his desk job at a hotel and signed on as a bell captain. He now works the 3:00 to 11:00 P.M. shift and spends the day with his daughters, ages five and two. "People around me are constantly interviewing for other jobs," he says, "telling me about the opportunities that come up. But when I think about my future, I look down and my future is running right around my feet."

A MATTER OF PRINCIPLE—CONRAD

While not time-clock double shifters, some partners try to balance job satisfaction, benefits, and work hours by switching off the various pieces. Conrad and his wife, Mary, are both dedicated to social causes; his strength is writing, hers is managing low-budget, understaffed operations. Conrad sees their family life as a "complex equation," based on "the reality of people who have basically opted out of the private profit-making sector." At the same time, he goes on, "we really believe in marriage, home, children, fidelity, solidity, bourgeois values . . . and those are very incompatible things." Their solution was to try to combine one job that met their political commitment with another one that offered such amenities as health insurance and a regular paycheck; and they had one more requirement: one of them would be with the children at the end of the school day.

Unlike most of the men, who felt their decisions about parenting had an economic price, Conrad found the opposite: "I'd say it's more the case that economic irresponsibility

took a toll on our parenting. . . . We were trying to balance reality—bills, economics, responsibilities—with very deep
passionate desires to do what we wanted to do. We did a lot
of projects that were downright uneconomical, and we were
living much closer to the financial edge than I am remotely
happy about, thinking back on it; 1992 was the hardest year
we ever experienced." That year Conrad was finishing a
book that took six more salaryless months than expected, so
Mary took a full-time job; although Conrad worked at home,
the pressure to get the book done was so intense that the
kids were put in day care. "The package just did not pan
out," he says of the setup. He hasn't done any writing of his
own since.

Like Don and Robert, Conrad talks about an equation.
"It's wearing to negotiate constantly and to reassess constantly what the equation is, that it is both workable and fair
and gives due space to all of the many competing agendas
that you have going on. I feel like I live by a code—not in
the moral sense, but in the sense of a deal I've struck with
my family—that no other man I know follows; and that
makes me feel like a freak sometimes. It makes me feel like
a sap sometimes. But," he adds emphatically, "there's such a
wonderful payoff for the investment."

The way he sees it, "You can make a trade-off by cutting
a hole or you can make the trade-off by setting a ceiling, and

I definitely am not working—and haven't been for many years—to my full mental capacity. I don't get that kind of satisfaction. Yet, if I have to choose between seeing my kids the way they are now, which I think is kids who are growing up with a really solid pair of adult relationships and who are doing great—they're socialized; they're not arrogant; they're not brats; they're graceful; they're talented—if I had to choose between that and another book, it's not even close."

Mood Swings—James

James and Fiona have been married for twelve years and have two children, seven and ten years old. They live in the Northwest in a house they have rebuilt with their own hands; they see themselves in the tradition of the pioneer spirit despite their trendy occupations. James, forty-six, makes commercials; Fiona, thirty-five, is in public relations. They have switched off being the primary breadwinner every couple of years. When they got married she was head of public relations for a large hotel chain. "Let me tell you," says James, who speaks with a kind of show-biz cockiness, "For five years we were at every resort for free. Then, when we had the baby, I said, 'What do you want to do?' and she said, 'I want to go back to work.' So I said, 'Well, I'll be here.' She thought I was bluffing. But there was no way in hell that I was going to have children and farm them out."

After three years, he goes on, "She said, 'I want to come home,' and I said, 'Fine, I'm outta here.' So I went. That is where we've been for several years, until just a couple of months ago when she was having trouble processing this endless grief cycle over her mother's sudden death; she said, 'I think I need to go back to work, honey.' I said, 'Fine, it's no problem.' Because to me the immediate thing was, 'Well, if you're working, I get the kids—great!' She's thrilled. We are very proud of the fact that we have a truly seamless sense of the adult responsibilities of a household with kids."

A VARIATION ON THE TWO-SHIFT THEME—DANIEL

Most double-shift setups bring the parents home from work to care for the children, but Daniel and Penny, both physicists, have turned the tables: they took turns bringing their baby, Ingrid, to work with them. "I stayed home with Penny and Ingrid for the first week," Daniel begins. "Then I went back to work and Penny stayed home with Ingrid for the rest of the first eight weeks. Then when she went back to work, we would divide the day so that Penny would go in to work early and I'd go in a little bit later, bringing Ingrid with me. I'd keep Ingrid in my office for the morning. At noon, we'd have lunch and I'd hand Ingrid over to Penny, and she would take her for the afternoon." And how did coworkers react? "People got so they really enjoyed having her around. But, of course, since we were the first to do this, there was a certain novelty." And how did his work go? "It was definitely distracting having Ingrid around. I was definitely getting less done than I normally do. I could make up some of it by doing extra work in the evening after Ingrid went to sleep. But to some extent it was a period where I wasn't as productive as I had been. But," he adds, "I was a whole lot more productive than if I hadn't been there at all. And if you think about what would have been involved in finding and training new people to replace me, that's disruptive and expensive, too."

Reverse double-shifting only worked for the first six months or so. Once Ingrid learned to crawl, Daniel explains, it was no longer practical to take her to work ("She would be totally miserable if she were in our offices with us now"). So they found a day-care program near the campus, but they still maintain a modified two-shift schedule. Daniel takes her in late in the morning and works late, while Penny starts early and picks Ingrid up in the early afternoon.

ONE PARENTAL UNIT WITH MANY JOBS—MARTIN

Martin is a big boisterous bear of a man. He asserts his opinions with the force of an Old Testament patriarch, and indeed his family setup looks like the classic division of labor with little trading off, but he sees what he and his wife have done as a mutual trading away of certain life experiences for the greater good of the "unit." His wife is at home caring for their nineteen-month-old baby and collecting material for a book she hopes to write about people's feelings about their favorite desserts; she also spends a great deal of time reading up on child rearing and briefing Martin when he comes home. He has his own computer-design business that demands a lot of attention and crisis-mode decision making, but he rejects the idea of a career track. "I'm an extremely ambitious person, but not in the way of simply getting to a higher rank in some sort of structure." He has a special understanding of where work fits in the value system he shares with his close friends. "We do work, we may even have vocations or avocations, but most of us consider it something you do to fulfill your goals. If our jobs give us value in the eyes of others, in the eyes of those who give us money or whatever, then we are able to do what we set out to do. In our case, it's have kids and a family life." Martin's priority is to contain his work within the weekly parameters of his religion and his own devotion to his family.

"Four days a week, Monday through Thursday, I wake up early so that I can play with the baby and hang out with my wife for maybe half an hour. Yesterday, for example, I got up at six, did some laundry, did some dishes, kinda snuck in, checked out . . . sort of woke up the baby. My wife woke up, we played, and had a great time. Then I go to work. No one expects me home till midnight. On Friday I get up early, go to work, come home at six, go to synagogue. No matter what, we have Friday night and Saturday." An Orthodox Jew, Martin considers Saturday the inviolate day of rest, but he is trying to add Sunday to his weekend. "It's a real risk I'm taking that could backfire. We're in a tough little business. None of my competitors take the weekend off."

A year later he was still holding on to his Sundays and had become a father for the second time. His business was booming and he concluded that his satisfaction as a family man had contributed to his performance as a businessman.

When asked about the division of labor in his family, he takes on a Talmudic tone. "Remember, we're not dealing with just me here; we're a unit. And our unit needs one of the people to be out working and schmoozing and taking out clients and whatever I do." He sees the unity of the "unit" in a very personal way: "I almost reject the term 'father.' For me there is no such thing as fathers without mothers... there's parents. We're the parents."

For Martin and many of the other men I talked to, a crucial factor in how burdensome the trade-offs feel is timing. "I had my first kid when I was thirty-six years old. My kid never got in my way, in the way of any experiences I wanted to have, any wild times I wanted to have. I never once said, Oh, you ruined my life and made me fat and out of shape; I was already plenty fat and out of shape by the time I got my kid.

If I'd had a child when I was nineteen, I bet I would have had a whole different attitude. Because that kid would have been an albatross around my neck, and I would have felt like I couldn't have traveled and couldn't have had fun."

A FINELY TUNED MACHINE—ANDREW

Andrew, thirty-two, has crafted a variation on the themes of downsizing ambition, shift scheduling, minimizing social life, and planning very carefully. He and his wife, Annabel, who is a management consultant, have two children—Freddie, four, and Mitch, fourteen months—and another on the way. He is a surgeon, though his lanky and laid-back presence is the opposite of the wired and wise-guy stereotype. But, he explains, he's not *that* kind of surgeon. "I chose orthopedics, which is, of all the surgeries, the most family-compatible, the most independent," he says. "It's mostly elective surgery. Your time is your own; you set your own schedule; you decide how much you want to work. I am a fourth-year resident now, so I don't take any more in-house calls. Essentially I come in at six o'clock in the morning, so I don't see the kids in the morning, but I'm usually done by four in the afternoon, sometimes earlier." Both he and Annabel are building their career plan toward a three-day workweek.

Andrew doesn't deny the appeal of work. "Work is a great place. Look at me. I wear pajamas all day. I get to operate, which is the most fun thing—I can't even tell you how much fun that is. We make jokes and listen to music in the operating room; then we go and eat lunch together. I would be lying to you if I said that I didn't love it."

His wife is equally committed to her job, but they have built their lives around time with their children, even if that means giving up golf ("I love golf, but I don't love it enough") or taking vacation weeks with the children separately. "The amazing thing is—and I think this is an amazing thing—that there have been almost no days that our children have gone without seeing us," Andrew says proudly. "I can tell you," he adds, "95 percent of my friends, male friends, never see their children during the week. They don't see them in the morning and they don't see them in the evening."

"We maximize our time," he sums up, outlining a typical day. "Because we are on very different time schedules," he explains, "we'll talk to each other two or three times during the day. She'll say, 'How's it going? How does the operating room look, da-da-da?' And I'll say, 'Well, it looks like I'm going to be done at three-thirty or four.' She'll say, 'OK, then I'm going to work a little later.' So we do that. And the next night maybe we'll both be home, or if I know I'm going to be late, she'll come home early."

As he describes this arrangement, Andrew catches himself. "I don't want to make it sound like a business, because I think—and I would say she would say so, too—we have a fantastic marriage. We're totally in love with each other, and we have a great time together. But we're very, very busy people, and we've had to structure it like a business."

And what does the business make? Time. Time to balance the equation. "We're not outrageously wealthy, but the issue is not really one of money, it's one of time," he concludes. "And we both love what we do and are very involved in it. But if we thought that there was a real problem with our marriage or with our kids, each of us would give up our jobs in a minute."

TELLING TIME

Each of these fathers has made hard choices based upon how he sees his priorities, and for the most part the choices have been framed as what arm or leg he could cut off the body of his own experience. Mixing and matching mostly unsatisfactory child-care arrangements is a persistently costly and anxiety-producing element. Many working couples allocate almost one entire salary to their children's caretaker. And at urban day-care centers, the cost for a preschooler can run higher than the tuition at most state universities, according to a recent study by the Children's Defense Fund. Most alarming, nearly five million children are regularly left unsupervised after school. Despite such statistics, not one of the men I interviewed questioned the social conditions or the economic premises behind the trade-offs they were forced to make: It is the American way. Time is money. Work and family are mutually incompatible. And school has to get out at three o'clock.

In the same way as travel is emblematic of how no amount of trading off arms and legs can create a satisfactory balance with certain kinds of work, the school clock symbolizes a whole category of unnecessary discomforts caused by some of the standard trade-offs that are assumed nonnegotiable. Just look at the contortions Nick and Martha went through, and imagine how different their workdays might have been had they been able to match flexible work hours with a more flexible notion of "when school gets out."

What if schools were open as a home base for working families on a variety of schedules? The facilities could be adapted to offer many of the services that each individual family is scrambling to patch together at a price that swallows up much of their income (in child care, after-school programs, fast food, second car). With those savings, parents would surely be in a position to defray some of the cost; they might even be more likely to become involved in programs for the kids by, say, committing a number of personal days a year to supervise activities, drive older kids to do errands, or be on call to organize backup groups on snow days.

Take this fantasy one step farther and imagine if every time someone said, "There has got to be a better way," fresh thinking would be forthcoming. It is encouraging and dramatic that the $200 million budget for federally funded after-school programs in 1998 was five times that of 1997; legislators got the message from their constituents that making more use of school facilities is a "better way" to support families. But it is not likely that enough innovative ways out of the school-day bind or any other bind—including the guilt over what they assume are personal failures that keeps parents from trying to mobilize for change—will come to the fore, so long as so many of the people who need them most are dancing as fast as they can just to get through the day on their own. And not questioning the conditions that keep them dancing.

CHAPTER FIVE

DREADED TAPE AND
GRINDING GEARS

There would be more sense in insisting on man's limitations because he cannot be a mother, than on a woman's because she can be.

—Elizabeth Cady Stanton, 1885

THE MAN WHO TALKS A BETTER LINE than he walks about wanting to be an equal partner can make a pretty persuasive case for the excuse that women have more options and more support for their choices, while men are met by obstacles in the workplace, in the culture, and from their peers.

In fact, though, men have more options than they may admit, including that of throwing up their hands.

The option to opt out trumps all others, and all the men I interviewed took advantage, to some degree, of the certain knowledge that no matter what family need it is—including prodding him to shape up—his wife would be, as one put it, "on top of it."

This situation sets up a playing field that is not only uneven, but mined with high explosives. Sometimes the only way to get past them is to go around. A therapist counseling a couple at loggerheads over her nagging and his opting out offered some homey wisdom about compromise and accommodation: "My mother told me one thing about marriage. She said, 'There are times when it's best to let two and two equal *five*.'"

This chapter is about understanding that equation. Every couple will have to decide for themselves whether they want to subscribe to such *Alice in Wonderland* mathematics. In any case, they will have to immerse themselves in a world where many of the elements are not what they seem and others aren't clear enough at this stage of the game to build a partnership on.

For one thing, it is not clear how much of the part of equal parenting a given man really wants to pick up—or even whether, in his mind, parenting includes all the other business of running a household. It is also not clear how much of the essential emotional expertise a man who has not learned it along the way *can* pick up. And it is not clear how much of the unending and thankless family maintenance skills he is prepared to learn. For him, moving toward equality is an awkward and sometimes painful expedition, every step a creaking and grinding of emotional gears. I call this rustiness the Grinding Gears.

The Grinding Gears have a protective function, too. Their rusty clanking is a warning to anyone around that making transitions from place to place or from task to task does not come naturally to most men. Don says he doesn't "feel bad about needing to be reminded to do things, because it seems to be a common pattern among men, at least men that I know. But," he adds, "it makes me wonder whether men are hard-wired to have the pause button constantly on."

The message is just as murky when a woman talks a good line about wanting to be an equal partner. There is plenty of support for her complaint that while men may extend a bit of noblesse oblige and help when asked, women are still taking on the lioness's share of the responsibility for the smooth running of family life—from keeping track of school projects, grandma's birthday, and the last tube of toothpaste, to managing adolescent moods and picking up on hurt feelings.

That responsibility pulses night and day, at work and at home, awake or asleep, in the back of her mind. Intertwined like a double helix of DNA with the litany of work demands and personal commitments, it forms the Dreaded Tape.

Like the Grinding Gears, the Dreaded Tape has a protective function, too, akin to wrapping oneself in the flag. The almost religious aura that surrounds the keeper of the home fires fends off all kinds of evil spirits, from second-guessers and critics, to the most terrifying of all—what might happen if someone who didn't know what they were doing took over.

It isn't clear how much of the masterminding and the assurance that things are being done in accordance with her revered "right away" most women are willing to relinquish.

Most disconcerting of all, it isn't clear—yet—whether it is possible for a family to function smoothly without everything being processed on a single tape through a single "administrator." Every family's experience will compute differently as partners write their own equation.

THE LAND OF DREADED TAPE AND GRINDING GEARS

The terms "Dreaded Tape" and "Grinding Gears" are my way of summarizing some of the differences that cause trouble between men and women as parents. They show up in the way we think and in the way we behave.

For a woman, the Dreaded Tape is the tormentor, the inner scold that keeps updating lists—lists of things to do, things to remember, things to worry about, things to remind others to do. Items from work are jumbled with items having to do with home, and they chatter on in her mind nonstop. The tape is more than a shopping list. We experience it as an umbrella of responsibility that requires surpassing organizational skills, expertise in many areas from medicine to arts and crafts, the ability to read minds, predict the future, and create harmony—often all at once. And if that weren't enough, there is one more responsibility: getting everyone else in the family to meet his or her responsibilities.

Men, in general, come to parenting and family life with less background noise, but also less sensitivity to context. Their approach is to compartmentalize experience and tasks, moving in as orderly a way as possible from one to the next. Grinding Gears describes the way men feel when they are forced to abandon this one-thing-at-a-time style for the more chaotic and piecemeal existence that is the heartbeat of family life. In the workplace it is more possible to impose an order on the day and complete one task or deal with one person before encountering the next; at home the only thing that can be counted on is the certainty that the unexpected will occur.

When the Dreaded Tape comes up against the Grinding Gears, women get impatient; they can't really understand how men can be so "slow" or "oblivious." For their part, men don't like being forced to strip their gears, and they resent the bossy know-it-all who is doing it.

Because women keep so many gears engaged at all times, they have less trouble than men moving in and out of very different circumstances. The renowned anthropologist Margaret Mead was a world-class gear shifter, according to her biographer Jane Howard, who marveled that she "managed to shift gears as often as she did, personally and professionally, without destroying her transmission." While Mead was a remarkable exception to any standard, millions of ordinary women keep many agendas running simultaneously, shifting among tasks and people at work and at home; in fact, given the range of their attentive radar that is regularly updating the Dreaded Tape, they never really leave home at all.

Quite literally, according to a recent analysis of commuting habits. Statisticians for *American Demographics* magazine tried to categorize a typical end-of-day ride for an average working woman. On the one hand, it could "count as a commute," they speculated, "but perhaps a school trip as well—and it could also be two shopping trips, if she stops to pick up dry cleaning and shop for dinner." A man's commute is much easier to track; it's "more likely to be a simple point-to-point journey."

"Transportation experts call the woman's ride a multiple-purpose trip, or 'trip chaining,'" the report explains. "What it means is that women on their way to or from work are more likely than men to be thinking about buying things and taking care of other people."

Even when they are technically off duty, the pattern is the same. John Carey, a social science researcher, studied viewing habits across America and found that women "are often doing something else while watching TV, e.g., they are preparing a meal, sorting laundry or reading a newspaper to catch up on the news. Curiously," he found, "few males reported that they engaged in other activities while watching TV."

Rather than feeling accomplished and efficient, though, busy women often feel penalized for having become so competent by being left holding the responsibility bag. They can do it, but they don't like shifting gears a thousand times a day at the behest of the Dreaded Tape.

Many of the men I talked to were dimly aware of the Dreaded Tape. While a few claimed that their thoughts about work were always in the background, none of them had a fully operational tape of their own going. They referred me to the Grinding Gears explanation—that they are built in such a way that their efforts to combine work and family put their transmission in jeopardy all the time. They simply can't shift gears as fast or as often as women do and therefore can't manage as much. These men seem to function most comfortably the way they drive to work, from point to point, with very little mental cruising from one demand to another; for them, every shift of gears is from zero to fifty.

For many, the most wrenching transition is "walking through the front door." Not to mention the difficulty of walking back out again. As one father told British journalist David Cohen plaintively, "When I head back to work after the weekend, I feel like I've been on an airplane, transported from one reality to another. I'm wrenched out of the bosom of the family and thrust into the hard-play of the battleground where I can't reveal any weakness. Then by the end of the week, when I'm killing without remorse, I've got to step over the threshold and become human again."

A less desperate anecdote comes from *Timeshifting: Creating More Time to Enjoy Your Life* by Dr. Stephan Rechtschaffen: "My father practiced his own personal ritual for shifting from work time to family time when he came home at night. After saying hello to my mother and the kids, he would always take a shower, no matter what hour it was. . . . My mother was sometimes furious about how late dinner was, but nothing could make him abandon his personal ritual. He was not truly home, he used to say, until he'd 'washed off the day.'"

"Compartmentalizing" is the word—recently popularized in connection with President Clinton's behavior—Don Conway-Long, an expert on masculinity, uses to describe why men have such a hard time shifting gears. "Men have this ability to separate off one aspect of our life and forget about all the others. For example, I have two offices. I teach at Webster and at Wash U, so I go from one school to the other, and I forget what I'm doing at the first when I am at the second. And when you're driving home, you're not thinking, 'What will I find on the other side of the door?' you're still thinking about work. And then you walk in and all of a sudden it's a completely different environment." But, he insists, this pattern is not bred in the bone; it is learned protective behavior. "It comes from the development of ego boundaries for men with which we protect ourselves from penetration—emotional penetration from the outside as well as the physical penetration of the homophobic image. The ego boundaries, the external armor, is what we're deliberately creating for ourselves in this culture in order to find out what it means to be masculine and to separate the feminine from us.

"Compartmentalizing is a serious problem for us, but," he adds, apparently well versed in the ambivalence such a suggestion would evoke, "it's not women's job to teach guys." Then he hits home. "Men know more about what it means to be a woman than about being a man. It's his job to use masculine willpower and begin opening up to other men and figuring things out." One of the first things men will need to figure out is the place of the Dreaded Tape in their own family dynamic.

THE JOYS OF DOING ONE THING AT A TIME—ANDREW

Andrew, the happy-go-lucky orthopedic surgeon, is well aware of the oppressiveness of his wife's Dreaded Tape, and nothing would make him happier than to share with her the sense of well-being he enjoys. Ironically, the compartmentalized contentment he describes is just what drives many wives, who feel it is achieved at the expense of *their* contentment, to distraction.

"I'm able to completely leave work when I leave work. Even though I have lots of stuff that I need to do in research and grants and all this other stuff, but I'm able to leave that behind and just be with my kids. Whereas my wife is always thinking about something that she has to get done; that's probably why she is slightly more efficient and conscientious than I am in terms of getting things done and planning ahead. The curse of that, I think, for her is that her mind is always working on all the other things that need to get done, whereas I tend to just kind of focus on the moment. As a result, I'm able to be a little less stressed than she is."

He wishes she could lighten up—maybe even compartmentalize a bit—but he sees how insidious cultural assumptions can be. "When we got married, everything was great; we were both working toward our careers. Then we had a child. All of a sudden there were things that needed to be done, you know, in terms of doctors appointments, getting play dates, school, this and that, da-da-da. She ended up doing everything. It sort of snuck up on us," he explains. "She assumed that role, and I sort of let her do it because we both were raised in that kind of environment." By the time they realized what was happening, Annabel had gotten very good at ... everything. Now, he points out with admiration, "she's really incredible at keeping everything in this bubble, from making sure that Freddie has the T-shirt he needs to bring in to school next Thursday to buying a birthday present. Like she'll go into a store and buy six birthday presents and wrap them all and put five of them away. She's phenomenally good at that. To be honest with you, she's much more conscientious about things like paying the bills, checking to make sure that everything's done—you know, this and that."

"This and that" includes shaping him up. "We reached a point—I can't really tell you at what point that was—where she was like going out of her mind and I was all relaxed, as I always am. I'm a very relaxed person. But she was going out of her mind and getting stressed, and she said, 'Wait a minute, you're not doing anything. You're not . . .'"

Then, in passing, he makes a crucial distinction that the Dreaded Tape doesn't recognize, between sharing parenting and sharing everything else. "I was always actively there and involved—you know what I mean, playing with the kids— but I wasn't even keeping the checkbook, I wasn't paying the bills, I wasn't . . ."

As soon as he got the picture, he went to work. "It started with the bill paying. I immediately found out that you could pay on-line, I got it all hooked up, I never have to write a check, I never have to address an envelope, put a stamp on, everything else. So that's completely streamlined all our bill paying. Then we started dividing things up. I'm in charge of the car, of the house, of anything that breaks, all the maintenance, any machinery. If anything goes wrong, I call the service people, that's my responsibility—unless she happens to be on vacation for the week and she can."

He takes doing his share very seriously. "I'm a very conscientious person myself, I like to think, and once I take it on, I just treat it like my job." But for all the jobs he takes on, the Dreaded Tape is not one of them. So, periodically his marching orders have to be updated. "There are definitely times where she'll kind of get frustrated and say, 'Look, I'm doing all these things: I'm doing all the thank-you notes, I'm doing all the clothes, I'm doing all the school stuff, I'm doing all the . . .' Like she'll get overwhelmed with something. So I'll take two new things on or two projects or I'll be in charge of, say, all our family trips." He is happy to assume new responsibilities, but the responsibility for knowing what needs to be assigned is not one of them.

Even so, I began to think after a couple of hours with Andrew, that if goodwill and dedication to a beloved partner's happiness are a powerful enough force, he and Annabel may be able to break through to a place where he furnishes his compartments with the wherewithal to give a little more forethought to the family's agenda and where she lets a few more chips fall where they may.

While Andrew is a beneficiary of the contribution the Dreaded Tape makes, he is also aware of its perils. "One thing that we both said from the time that our oldest son was six months was this is the way it has to be—if you're with the kids, you can't plan on doing anything," he explains. "Don't plan on getting X, Y, and Z done; otherwise you'll get frustrated and you'll not enjoy it and everything else. I think we've both done that." But, he adds, "I think I'm a little better at that than she is."

As Good As It Gets

Nick and Martha have been at it a good fifteen years longer than Andrew and Annabel, and they started from a very clear commitment to sharing everything in their marriage. So much so that it appears at first that they have even found a way to share the Dreaded Tape. They set such an egalitarian standard that they have alternated the last names of their three children, meaning the middle one has Martha's last name. (Mary Rose likes the distinction of having her own last name, Nick believes, and the practice is not as disruptive as it might seem. "Schools deal with so many situations these days—hyphenated names, divorce and remarriage—that I don't think it's as big a deal as it used to be. The doctor's office is the only one that seems to screw up.")

Yet the drone of the Dreaded Tape is still louder on Martha's side. "I keep track of the money," says Nick, "but she has a sense that I'm faking it; you know, 'Oh, we'll make it next month,' then we won't," he admits. "Things got pretty bad when we were sharing one job; the money just wouldn't sustain it. It was an emergency, really. We needed another job and we needed it quickly." Someone had to take charge. "Martha just got on the phone and made a call to her old paper and said, 'Got any work?' And they said, 'Yeah.' And it was very hard for her. It felt like going backwards, seeing the old characters from your past and they are now your boss. I have to credit her; I couldn't have gone back to my old paper; I would've been drinking scotch all the way to work."

Because they are committed to the egalitarian model, Nick and Martha's experience highlights the question underlying the mixed feelings both have about the Dreaded Tape, a question that cannot yet be answered: Can a busy family manage without the assurance that some*one* is "on top of things"? Or, to put it another way, can the Dreaded Tape be shared?

The question presupposes a man who really wants to go "all the way" on this one.

MADAME GENERAL

A sneaking suspicion that they are getting away with something may explain the inkling I got in the course of talking to Andrew and Nick and many of the others that they were becoming increasingly anxious about whether I would share our discussion with their wives. They never actually said so—in fact, many said the opposite, "Oh, you'll have to ask my wife about that, but I think she would say I'm doing a pretty good job"—but I couldn't help sensing that the prospect made them uncomfortable.

Maybe the husbands didn't want the wives to hear themselves being cast, as they regularly were (though never in so many words) as the Generals. Maybe they were afraid that they wouldn't get as good a grade from the General as they gave themselves, or maybe they didn't want the General to know how much control she had or to know that *they* know.

For their part, the Generals roll their eyes. Each points out how, typically, the man who proudly claims he does the grocery shopping is usually clutching a list made by his wife. The Generals get together over coffee and agree that for the purposes of getting things done right, they should be married to each other. They even say this in front of their husbands. Don recalls "settings where we've been having dinner with another couple and the wives are having a conversation about us, like we're not there, but we're sitting there. 'Don't you hate it when he . . .' 'Yeah, I have to ask him to do whatever all the time.'"

And they do it in print. Pat Schroeder, former congresswoman from Colorado, recalls that her very supportive husband, Jim, was once asked how her being in Congress had changed his life, to which he had responded that he had to do more things like taking the children to the pediatrician. Upon hearing this she "immediately ran to the House cloakroom and called him" she writes in her memoir, *24 Years of House*

Work... And the Place Is Still a Mess. "'For $500,' I asked him, 'what is the name of the children's pediatrician?' Knowing he was busted, he coughed and said, 'Oh, I was misquoted.' Jim was way ahead of his time, but he wasn't Mr. Mom," she concludes.

As any educator knows, sarcasm is not a useful teaching tool; it only engenders resentment and resistance. By the same token, "the dog ate my homework... again" is the most exasperating of excuses. So, while it may be worth being laughed at, not to have to do it, no one likes to be laughed at. It may be more fun to laugh at them than to get them to do it, but no one really likes to be a nag. Can men and women change their ways?

HIS BRAIN / HER BRAIN

Syndicated columnist Dianne Hales began an article on what is known about brain function with a familiar scenario: "After 20 years of marriage, my husband still doesn't understand me. Why, he wants to know, am I always doing three things at once? Why do hokey old movies make me cry? Why do I mull things over (and over) rather than rushing into action? How is it that I am never at a loss for words—or that I can zero in on the mustard when he's been scanning the refrigerator shelves for five minutes? Why do I keep turning down the volume when he's just turned it up? And how come I can recall the names of the couple we met years ago in Hawaii when he can't?

"Now I know what to tell him: It's my brain."

By the same token, she might have asked why her husband can't watch television and discuss the children's school problems at the same time, or why he won't look at her when she is crying or yelling, or why he keeps on driving even after he knows he is lost, or why he can read in the dark, and why he never notices when she has moved all the furniture in the living room around, and why in heaven's name he never picks up on her moods.

The answer would be the same: It's his brain.

Of the many differences identified by scientific studies and enumerated by Hales in her article, some are especially pertinent to understanding the Dreaded Tape and the Grinding Gears and much else that is going on. Of course, the differences are not immutable and like all gender distinctions, they focus on extremes, while most men and women find themselves in the middle. Still, it does help to recognize "typical" behaviors of one gender that can appear so aberrant to the other.

- Men use specific parts of the brain for specific tasks, enabling them to focus intently; women use more of their brain for the same task, enabling them to pick up "cross talk" between the emotional and the rational side.

- Men are wired for action and aggression, women for symbolic expression like words and gestures.
- Men are better at seeing 3-D, women at "disembedding"—noticing when one of several objects in a field has been changed.
- Men have sharper vision in low light; women have more acute hearing.
- Men can't remember events as well as women who seem to do so by "tagging" things that happen with an emotional cue.
- Women make more connections than men; hence, they are more intuitive; men are more literal.

Thus, the same information can travel a different path and deliver a different message to men and to women. Joan Meyers-Levy, a professor of marketing, used her findings about perception to help the advertising community tailor its messages to different groups. Much of her advice stems from what she has found about men's inclination to address problems by eliminating extraneous elements and focusing in on one or two features (as opposed to women's efforts to integrate the disparate elements into a solution).

She maintains that subtlety—mountain scenery to suggest refreshing taste in a beer ad, say—is lost on men; to be effective the ad must focus on the product and avoid mixing messages that leave men confused and turned off. For women, the opposite is true; their responses are enhanced by atmospheric cues.

The same response mechanism explains why men often seem to shut down emotionally in an intense face-to-face encounter and do so much better at a remove, on the phone, for example. It's a reaction to "emotional overload." Meyers-Levy's theory suggests that a man simply can't process nonverbal information (the expression and body language of the person addressing him) and verbal information at the same time. "Can't" may be too strong; as thousands of survivors of brain damage demonstrate, the brain can find ways to accommodate many challenges, but unchallenged, the path of least resistance quickly becomes an institution.

My favorite summary of the assumptions the genders have built up about each other was circulated on the internet and read by U.S. District Judge Thomas Penfield Jackson at—of all places—the Microsoft monopoly trial. When both women and men were asked what gender would be most appropriate for computers, among the reasons the women gave for voting "masculine" were:

1. *In order to get their attention, you have to turn them on.*
2. *They have a lot of data, but they are still clueless.*
3. *Most of the time, they are the problem.*

The men were just as convinced that computers should be female, because

1. No one but the Creator understands their internal logic.

2. The native language they use to communicate with other computers is incomprehensible to everyone else.

3. Even your smallest mistakes are stored in long-term memory for later retrieval.

The trouble with laughing at this bit of cyberhumor is that it seems to buy into biology-is-destiny thinking, which delivers such gems as conservative economist Francis Fukuyama's pronouncement in *Foreign Affairs* that "The basic social problem that any society faces is to control the aggressive tendencies of its young men." (As if society weren't *creating* those "tendencies.")

Evolution has produced some instructive models, though. Male Emperor penguins are nature's most egalitarian fathers; they hatch their offspring single-handedly, wasting their own bodies while keeping the eggs warm under a droopy stomach fold; meanwhile, the female rebuilds the strength lost in growing the eggs. The behavior of the eastern bluebird is especially intriguing in that it suggests that biology can offer more than one destiny. Anne Fausto-Sterling, a professor at Brown, has observed that "male birds of this species broker sex in exchange for defending scarce nesting sites. But what happens when there are plenty of places to nest? The female doesn't need to exchange sex for lodging. Under these circumstances, male bluebirds change strategies. They help females feed their babies." The bluebird experience suggests to Fausto-Sterling that we might do well to "think of adaptability, or plasticity, rather than specific behavior, as being under genetic control. In fact," she concludes, "geneticists have evolved sufficient data showing that plasticity is a trait under genetic control, and can evolve via natural selection."

The adaptable bluebirds remind me of a fellow I heard about whose family assignment was cooking. When he went away on a business trip, he left the requisite number of meals wrapped up in the freezer. He was only doing what comes naturally, he told a friend. "In the old days, the men would go off and slaughter a few infidels to prove they loved their families. Today we freeze a couple of casseroles."

INTIMACY, EMPATHY, AND "AW, SHUCKS"

While physiologists explore gender differences in the brain, psychologists are looking at how men and women develop emotionally. "Differing stances toward intimacy signify deeper disparities between the sexes," in the view of Carol Gilligan, professor of Gender Studies at Harvard who wrote the groundbreaking study of girls' moral development, *In A Different Voice*. "Young boys take pride in independence and are

threatened by anything that might compromise their autonomy," Gilligan says, "while young girls tend to experience
themselves as part of a network of relationships and are threatened by anything that might rupture these connections."

"Boys, as they mature, must learn to connect, girls to
separate," adds Kathleen White, a psychologist at Boston
University. "The more comfortable a husband is with intimacy, Dr. White's research shows, the more satisfied with
the marriage the wife is likely to be," concludes psychology
writer Daniel Goleman.

The tension between connection and autonomy is played
out in the contradictions between the Dreaded Tape, so
threaded with nuances of family behavior and emotions, and
the Grinding Gears, which creak and groan when family demands impinge on autonomy.

The leaders of the Promise Keepers—the revival movement of men seeking to reestablish traditional family values
that staged a gigantic march on Washington in 1997—are
measuring the distance most men need to go in order to
hook up with family life. Their recent publications report on
patterns that have emerged in discussion groups all over the
country. Participants claim they want intimacy but find
closeness threatening; they connect by asking questions, not
sharing experiences; and, when confronted with a loved
one's problem, they are less inclined to show sympathy than
to feel compelled to come up with a solution.

The connection between intimacy and problem solving may not be readily apparent, but if intimacy is the core of any marriage, cooperative problem solving is the paramount skill and a great source of satisfaction and sharing in the new egalitarian style. Once upon a time it was possible to have one without the other. Andrew recalls a wedding toast that encapsulates the situation he grew up in. "The fellow, who must have been in his seventies, got up and said, 'I want to give you some advice: When my wife and I were married, we decided right away that she would be in charge of all the day-to-day decisions, and I would be in charge of the really big important decisions. And I'm happy to report that after fifty years of marriage, I've yet to make a decision.' Everyone laughed," he adds, shaking his head. He and Annabel do things very differently. "We've had our rough points, where Annabel has been near tears because she's been overwhelmed by things, not really angry with me but kind of 'You've got to help me out here because something's not working.' Then we break it down and see why it's not working. We both are good problem solvers. That, I think, is both of our strength."

DEEDS NOT WORDS—RALPH AND PHILIP

Ralph can't imagine getting the kind of satisfaction Andrew experiences from talking things through with his wife, Cassie. He knows she is disappointed with his approach, but he thinks it may be impossible to go against his upbringing. "Men are brought up explicitly to say nothing. You shouldn't complain unless you're going to fix the problem. My father must have said that to me five hundred times," he begins. Talk is not a solution; it's another problem. "When I talk about problems that I can't resolve, I get less and less happy, more and more miserable. I don't feel better afterward. And I think that's the root of huge amounts of conflict between men and women. Women want to talk, and they feel better afterward, and the man feels wretched," he suggests. "If he tries to fix the situation, she says, 'I didn't want you to *do* anything about it, I just . . .' It may go back to the days when the men went out and tried to slay a woolly mammoth or something." He is aware of Cassie's expectations but can't seem to meet them. "I try to beat back this reflex to react with a proposed solution to the problem. And my wife is incredibly frustrated if I do that, and she's also incredibly frustrated if she doesn't talk about a problem. But I think the way women are psychologically on this issue is in the popular culture now believed to be the way everyone should be. And it's just really hard for men to be that way."

Philip knows whereof Ralph speaks. The way he tells it, problem solving is not only a function of communication styles, but of intimacy styles. His Grinding-Gears approach (one thing at a time, preferably something that can be acted upon and disposed of then and there) seems totally incompatible with his wife's Dreaded-Tape approach (cross-refer precedents and causes, look at consequences, assign responsibility, and keep track of progress). "I tend to be proactive," he says. "I want to figure out how to solve it; Helen tends to be reactive—she's still living the problem in her mind and trying to express it, to communicate it." His objective is to move toward a solution as quickly as possible and "move past the immediate feeling of pain, which is associated with any kind of problematic situation." Helen, meanwhile, wants to stay there for a while and confirm a sense of intimacy. "She turns a problem into a communal experience," he concludes. "She wants empathy. But for me it's confusing to have someone sort of invite you into their pain. Because it causes me pain. And talking about it just reminds me over and over of how painful it is. For me, the idea is to suppress the pain, make it go away. You do that by trying to ignore it or by dealing with it in some proactive fashion."

Words in general are problematic for Philip. Ironically, he is stunningly articulate when he tries to explain why. "I want everything to be sort of at face value. It makes the world a whole lot easier to deal with if you can say, 'Let's just define this as this and let's work it out on that level and get it done.' With Helen there are linkages between the message that she is giving and other things she has feelings about regarding every aspect of our relationship. There's always a way to link what's in the present to something that exists in the history of the relationship. I tend to delink present experiences from other things in past experience."

For Philip, even affection is "delinked" from language; it is "just part of the ground of existence, a given: I loved you yesterday and I love you today and nothing has changed." He can't speak to Helen's "reality" which is "constructed out of words; it's a symbolic reality that needs to be rebuilt or patched up every single day by describing it or else it's going to dissipate. That's the way I see a lot of relationships she has with her friends. I can see the world just being built by the conversation that they're having."

Philip's description of the language dichotomy between himself and his wife echoes the insight of clinical psychologist Ronald Levant in connection with that other crucial arena of communication—sex. He describes an impasse between a husband and wife who came to him for therapy: "'We never talk,' she said. 'All we do is exchange information.' 'I don't know what she wants from me,' he said. 'I don't have anything to say.' Stalemate. To her, sex was an expression of closeness and connectedness. She didn't feel close to him; therefore, she wasn't comfortable having sex. To him, sex was a route to closeness and connectedness—his only route. What did talking have to do with having sex?"

After some thought, Philip has an insight. "I guess a lot of these things have to do with the way that I deal with emotionally charged situations." He begins to see his response as protective. "I like to control my inner space. I construct an edifice and I don't want to subject it to modification. It gets worked on when I am reflective. But I don't put it out there on the line in every conversation that I have."

A Wall of Silence

Since sharing doubts and fears is so inimical to most men, it is no surprise that they aren't much good at making emotional connections with one another. Many spoke to me of a good friend with whom he could talk about his kids' progress but not about their problems. Paul, who is a scriptwriter, collaborates with a man who has an infant daughter not much older than Paul's son, Jacob. "We talk about practical things, about when they do certain things like roll over or crawling. We talk about how it's hard to balance work and home and how it's important to make time to help our wives but sometimes they get angry if we need to work a little later. So it's more practical things. but he's not an emotional person, keeps a lid on his emotions. I don't really know any guys who have kids who are able to discuss their emotions."

Here's how fragile and tentative the baby steps toward male intimacy felt to Will Glennon, who described in *New*

Moon Network (a magazine for parents of girls), how a man like him might reach out during an unusual golf game with a friend. "And on the fourth hole, up in the tee box, we say, 'Jim, you know, I was thinking about my daughter the other day...' And you have a little 10-minute conversation, and you really get to share some stuff. And then you tee off quickly and get the hell out of there, so you can recover your composure! Because this is not stuff you're comfortable with, and it takes a while to get used to it."

Bottling up feelings is most definitely a male thing. But it may be that the men and women who are changing so many other aspects of their lives are also pioneers in emotional fluency. A recent experiment by psychologist Ann Kring and researcher Albert H. Gordon at Vanderbilt University exposed 110 men and women to a range of film clips, from comedies to horror and tragedy, and monitored their responses. Both men and women described similar reactions, but the women displayed their feelings with facial expressions, while the men's expressions of sadness, fear, happiness, disgust were only visible on the screen of a gadget that measures sweaty palms. The most interesting finding, though, was that the participants, both men and women, who were most emotionally demonstrative were those who responded in a questionnaire that they felt less governed by the unwritten rules about gender behavior and more free to express themselves however they please.

SHIFTING GEARS, BUT RUNNING
ON A BORROWED TAPE

Most men are used to calling upon their wives, and through them the larger community of women, when it comes to those messy human problems that defy clear-cut—"proactive," to use Philip's word—solutions. That vast universe of anxiety, ambivalence, partial success, and partial failure encompasses most concerns about children.

Alan describes an important decision that he and his wife made which involved enrolling their son in a special class that combined third and fourth grade or leaving him in the standard sequence. They had to make a determination about the program's value and factor in their understanding of their son's needs, personality, and future. They were agonizing over the question, worried that they would make a "wrong" decision; the awareness that they would probably never know for sure only made for more pressure.

"We'd talk about it between ourselves a lot. I also get the benefit of the advice that Catherine collected through *her* friends. She has many more friends that she talks to about the kids and shares stories with about what works and what doesn't work than I have. I haven't talked about it with any of my male friends." Then, while they were still sorting things out, they were invited to the home of some friends. "There were three couples. One had a kid in fourth grade, so they have made the decision. The other has a kid in second grade, so they will be making the decision along with us. The subject came up, and the three women talked, and the three men kind of listened."

There is another reason, besides their discomfort with uncertainty and self-doubt, that these fathers are taking their cues from their wives. The truth of the matter is that in the absence of role models for the kind of fatherhood they are trying to achieve, most men shape their behavior around what they see of motherhood. Even though Robert spent six months at home with his newborn son, he was never confident that he had all the moves down. If he "had a bad day with the baby or thought, Gee, I've just done something wrong," he'd call his wife at her office. "Just for the reassurance that I hadn't screwed up."

Even though Peter did homework with his nine-year-old son as often as his wife did, when Arthur began to show signs of attention deficit disorder, it was his wife who "saw it, addressed it." His contribution "to the extent that I did a good job, it was that I did a good job of letting her lead the way."

And Daniel, who is, by all known measures, a completely co–primary caregiver (he even sought out, found, and interviewed and hired a baby-sitter without involving his wife), acknowledges that "more than anything I try to identify with and model myself after what I see Penny doing. If I notice her doing something with Ingrid that Ingrid seems to like that I don't do, I'll say, maybe I should do that more. I try to pick up things from her."

The search for models that will help parents get past some of the psychological barriers to loving collaboration and beyond debates over the meaning of variations in male and female wiring may lead not to marriage manuals and business partnerships but to another relationship in the family: to the parent-child dynamic, which is, when all is said and done, at the heart of the matter.

After all, the main reason so many fathers are going through all the hassle of going against type is because they want to achieve the kind of connection with another part of human experience and with another human being that they can only imagine. They want to learn the language of intimacy and trust. They know as deeply as anyone can know anything that getting there is worth whatever it takes. That certainty is fueling the revolution they are making.

Philip's face lights up when he talks about the wonder of interacting with his kids. "There's nothing more magical to me than getting down at their level and listening to what they're trying to tell me. Because they are not only articulating something that's important to them, but they are figuring out how to do it as they are doing it. I love watching the process and I want to help them be better at it. I feel so utterly connected with them and I want to say, 'What is it you feel? I want to watch you express it and figure out how to express it, and I'm going to feel such a sense of accomplishment when I know you have successfully completed that transaction.'"

It may be easier to respond with joy to a relationship with one's children than to go against eons of social convention with one's partner. After radiating the delight of talking about his kids, Philip's expression clouds over with a sad realization. "Why I don't do that with Helen, I don't know. It's funny, but I find it easier to listen to my children than to listen to my wife."

The answer to his dilemma may be closer to home than Philip knows. Good parents, like Philip, do all they can to foster trust, goodwill, and tolerance in their dealings with their kids by guiding where they can, supporting where they can't, and letting them learn from their own mistakes. The same compact just might work between the grown-ups as well.

CHAPTER SIX

WHAT'S FAIR IS FAIR—SEZ WHO?

Helping vs. Sharing

This is the age of negotiation in marriage: Who takes off work when a child is sick? Who handles the family finances? Who pays for the movie?... Marriages that survive do so not because of luck... but because of hard work and skill.

—*The Washington Post,* March 25, 1998, Part four of "Reality Check/The Gender Revolution"

LIKE THE WOMEN WHO WENT BEFORE THEM into the work-family unknown, the male jugglers are learning to deal with conflicting priorities and new working relationships. Many are also confronting some more mundane challenges for the first time: Once the proud Little League coach gets home from practice, full of fatherly satisfaction, there is still laundry to be done. Once a toddler's bath and bedtime stories have been accomplished, someone still has to have gotten the supplies for a third-grader's dinosaur project and arranged a replacement for the baby-sitter who has called in sick. "Shit work" is the inelegant term for the messy, goal-defying, unpredictable business of scrambling to manage the care and feeding of four or five or six people with vastly different needs and agendas. It involves being ready to think backwards, forwards, and sideways at all times. Typically, this is the province of the Dreaded Tape.

The more men try to take on, the better acquainted they become with the by-products of leading a double life that women are all too familiar with. For both, resentment—at the obstacles, at the enormity of the undertaking, at each other—is rampant. And increasingly, for men as well as women, guilt—over the half-done, the ineptly done, the left undone—is a constant companion.

There is an important distinction, though, between the experience of the women of the seventies and today's fathers. While women in all walks of life—not just the secretaries in the typing pool—were demanding release from shit work, both at work and at home, their male counterparts in the struggle for a balance are in effect putting themselves in the way of it. By the standards of conventional wisdom, what women were pushing for was a step up, what men are taking on is in many ways a step down.

"Helping"—the *spécialité* of the Grinding Gears—is a male way of keeping his dignity while honoring his commitments. It also enables both sides to retain an important kind of power: his to opt out and hers to pass judgment. It gets him off the hook and it preserves the authority of Mommy's Rules. But it doesn't make either party feel good.

To make matters worse, the egalitarian impulse that got working parents to this point in the first place doesn't always work in their favor. The more their daily lives are alike, the more likely that comparisons—Who is bringing in more money? Who is doing more for the family? Who is the better parent? Who has it easier?—heat up, according to psychiatrist Terry A. Kupers. "When his turf was the world of work and hers the home," he points out, "there was less need to compete."

The competition can be oh, so subtle. James, who appears to be genuinely comfortable in terms of trading back and forth roles in the family, seems to have some trouble trading in the macho impulse to be the best, to win, even while sharing. In our interview, he mentioned several times that his wife, Fiona, concedes (lovingly, of course) that he is better at "mothering" than she and that he is also better at the dollars and cents of food shopping. Finally, he went on at some length about what he and Fiona feel is the only problem in their marriage: *her* PMS!

Acid and bile were not on the menu back in the days when grocery shopping was fun and home was where you put your feet up. Before kids.

Newlyweds—raised in an increasingly egalitarian world—are not prepared for parenthood to turn lover into horse trader or partner into oppressor or helpmate into rival. What, they wonder, is happening to their marriage?

For one thing, the stakes have gotten very high. Carter describes the worst moments as a kind of catch-22: "We've had arguments where I think we would have ended the relationship had Jessica not been in the picture, but on the other hand, to a large extent these arguments are a result of our caring for Jessica."

One wonders how any two people carrying so much baggage ever get the dishes done, since they can't even establish the most basic workplace conditions: trust (on the woman's part) that the job will get done (her way?) and understanding (on the man's part) that it needs to be done (by him? and just then?). But somehow they do.

NEGOTIATE, NEGOTIATE, NEGOTIATE

A couple's success depends on how they meet the challenge to be "fair," how they factor highfalutin notions like teamwork and responsibility and "what's right" into mundane—but decidedly not minor—calculations, and how they distribute the apples and oranges of meal planning and moral education, laundry and life-management. If one person makes the pediatrician appointment and keeps track of the inoculations, and the other goes to those appointments, is one more responsible than the other? Is one doing more than his or her share? If one is strict and the other is a pushover, does that mean that the strict one has to do all the disciplinary heavy lifting? Or that the softie is disloyal?

That is why experts in family dynamics are emphasizing the importance of developing negotiating skills. Those couples I found who were most successful in making an allocation of tasks and responsibilities that felt fair to both parties were those who understood how *not* simple the negotiation is, and were aware of the need, as one father put it, "to keep adapting."

Edward T. Hall, an anthropologist who has written books for American businesspeople about to encounter their Asian counterparts, has a lot of experience with the mischief that can be caused, right at the start, by a language barrier. To get around it, he has come up with the notion of "contexting"— figuring out the unspoken information and assumptions behind a given statement—between cultures. "Ordinarily, people make these adjustments automatically in their own country," he says, "but in other countries their messages frequently miss the target." For all intents and purposes, fathers and mothers are coming to family life from very different countries, and the terrain they are entering looks different as a result.

The miscues between East and West may be about eye contact perceived as presumption on the Asian side and smiles perceived as acquiescence on the American side. Closer to home, where the land of the Dreaded Tape meets the land of the Grinding Gears, "pick up the living room" could mean "pile up the stray magazines and gather up the gummy coffee cups," or it could mean "vacuum the rug and polish the table." Does "take the kids for the afternoon" mean "get them new sneakers and try to lure them into the library for the science enrichment program"? Or does it mean "keep an eye on them while you catch up on some work"?

Two Different Worlds

Many of the men I spoke to felt that their partnership worked best when each had firsthand familiarity with the context of their partner's life and with the rhythm of commuting between two worlds. In this respect, the nitty-gritty of the household can be a tie that binds. Daniel thinks he and Penny have the perfect mix. "I think neither of us would be very well cut out to be a full-time parent. I think either one of us would burn out in a couple of weeks if we were at home all day with Ingrid. We're just so happy that we can be coparents with Ingrid and have our jobs, too."

Those who are trying to equalize just one side of more traditional spheres of influence find the context much harder to access. When a woman has been managing a home all day, the Dreaded Tape is deafening by dinnertime. When a man has been single-mindedly focused on the workaday world, reentering the family process can strip his gears.

Philip, whose wife has not worked outside the home for several years, often finds himself in a lose-lose situation the minute he walks through the door. Even though he and Helen have been trying to assign him a share of household tasks that can be done at night and over weekends, he feels he is getting more than his share of criticism. "When I am accused that I haven't lived up to my side of the bargain, I say, 'What do you want from me? I only have two hours a day when I am home at night. Look what I give. I can't do anything during the hours I'm at work; I'm engaged a hundred percent while I'm at work.' I go through the recitation, every hour of the day, what I'm doing and how I'm spending my time. At the end of the day, I've had enough of the stress and tensions of getting things done."

From his wife's point of view, his has been an orderly, if pressured day, while hers has been chaos. "Sometimes she'll say, 'Well, you've had an hour on the train to relax. I, on the other hand, have been here all day long. I haven't had a break from the kids all day long,'" by which she also means, as Philip sees it, that she needs "to spend some time communicating with me at night, because she hasn't had the opportunity to really do it on an adult level all day long." He, on the other hand, is coming from another end of the earth. "For me it's sometimes a matter of wanting to shut down as many systems as possible when I get home at night. It's unfair, but I'm reacting to my own needs as well as being insensitive."

"The truth of the matter," he concludes, "is that both of us are experiencing different kinds of stress in different kinds of ways."

Helen has begun to look for a job. Philip knows that she is worried that things will be harder in terms of all the household tasks that will need to be done at night and on weekends, but he hopes for more understanding. "There have been a couple of occasions when she has had to go to a conference in the city. She went on the train in the morning and came home on the train at night. She says, 'My god, how do you do that every day?' But I haven't had the presence of mind to remind her of those experiences when we're in the middle of arguing about who is doing what."

Paul, who has only been in the father game for eight months (during which time his wife, Beth, has been on maternity leave), found being Beth's conduit to the outside world a turnoff. "I would come home, and I didn't want to talk about my day with her, but she needed to connect with me. We were just relating through the baby instead of through each other. We got into a little rut where we weren't really talking and we weren't being romantic—I wasn't like really kissing her and I wasn't really like telling her I loved her. I was becoming emotionally remote. Like my father."

Robert, who stayed home for almost a year after the birth of their second child, is in the unusual position—for a man—of seeing things from Beth's perspective. For three months both he and his wife were full-time parents, and he saw what life without even one emissary to the outside world in the family is like. "When you're both not coming home from work every day, your conversation is all about the kids and family and all of that, which is fine—obviously there is plenty to deal with—but it takes a dimension away from just how you relate to each other. You miss relationships with people at work. You don't have anything to complain about from work. You don't have anything that you've accomplished at work. You're just kind of living at home; you have accomplishments and complaints dealing with that, but I don't think I ever envisioned that I'd be sitting around with adults having conversations about sleep and potty training and all that kind of stuff."

Tillie's dad, Ralph, the million-mile-a-year traveler, who managed at great effort to get to his daughter's fifth birthday party, just about kills himself trying to make a seamless transition from those grueling business trips. But he doesn't really understand how far away he has been or how far away he remains from the fabric—the intimate dailiness that messing and cleaning up builds—of his family's life.

He has made an ironclad commitment that "No matter where I've been or what time I get home, we must have a family outing every Saturday and every Sunday. No matter how tired I am. No matter what." But his efforts to compensate for an untenable situation don't address the needs of his wife, who stays home with the children and has had to handle everything from insurance bills to parents' night while he was away. They are in a lose-lose stand off. "I get angry," he admits, "because I think the level of blame would be appropriate if I was away by choice, if I preferred being away to being at home. But the reverse is true, and so I feel as much of a victim of the situation as anyone else and yet I have to take the blame for not being able to spend more time with my family."

CLEANING UP AFTER OTHER PEOPLE

One participant in a *Ladies' Home Journal* roundtable saw the distance between his world and her world in very concrete terms. "She always complains, 'He always leaves the toilet seat up. Why doesn't he put it down for me?' Why," he wanted to know, "doesn't *she* put it *up* for me? Fair is fair."

But what exactly *is* "fair"?

The crucible of equity is in the details—of housework.

Housework is the monster in the cupboard that won't go away. No matter how many gadgets and systems are invented, the sorcerer's apprentice makes no headway. A 1972 study by an international team of social scientists cited by Carol Tavris and Carole Wade in their book, *The Longest War*, confirmed this sad fact. After enlisting two thousand participants in twelve countries to keep a detailed diary of housework, they found that "the average woman in Osnabrück, West Germany, has all the appliances she wants, yet she spends as much time doing housework—within a minute—as a wife in Kragujevac, Yugoslavia, who still draws water from a well."

Even when there is plenty of paid help, the job doesn't vanish from her radar screen. It just becomes once removed, as background noise of the Dreaded Tape—which is certainly less exhausting but not necessarily less stressful. For one thing, finding, hiring, training, monitoring, assigning, and replacing the people who help is one more very time-consuming responsibility. Paying someone to do the cooking doesn't relieve the pressure to plan the meal; having someone to care for the children doesn't lift the urgency of making sure that person shows up. Not doing it by oneself doesn't diminish the burden of making it happen. Certainly "help" helps immeasurably, but it doesn't level the playing field. The underlying dynamic is what counts.

To their credit, men are doing more of the housework. Every year a minute or two is added to the average number of hours they spend doing chores (it is up by about an hour over the past twenty years—2.2 hours on workdays and 4.2 on nonworkdays in 1997), and for the most part those minutes come off the number of hours that women are doing (down from 3.7 to 3.1 hours on workdays and from 7.2 to 6.1 on nonworkdays).

They do it, but in their hearts, most fathers don't consider housework a real part of their job description. They can get all fired up over the honorable work of what they define as equal parenting—which usually extends to some KP—but they are less enthusiastic about the part of the deal that involves the culturally demeaned business of cleaning up after others. When the *Washington Post*, the Kaiser Family Foundation, and Harvard University surveyed Americans "on gender," they found that men and women overwhelmingly agree (93 percent) that "the care of children should be shared equally by both parents." But the same study confirmed that women spend much more time doing food shopping, taking children to appointments, paying the bills, cooking, washing clothes, and cleaning house.

Here is one man's particularly honest description of the way things are: "'It's much more equal in what I do with Pete than in the house. I enjoy looking after him; it's more fun than washing dishes or even than putting them in the dishwasher, which I'm still not very good at. I'm lazy about housework and stuff like that, and Rachel is compulsive enough that if it doesn't get done, she'll do it. And I take advantage of that.'"

Sociologist Kathleen Gerson quotes this father in her book *No Man's Land* as an example of the group she calls "mothers' helpers." They take the role of "reactor rather than initiator." After interviewing 138 men she found that "most involved fathers concluded that being a mother's helper holds fewer drawbacks and offers enough rewards to make it the more attractive option." That leaves, as more work for mother, "the job of seeing that tasks are distributed equitably—or of making sure they get done at all."

An item in *American Baby* magazine gives a glimpse of how much effort women invest in cajoling men into doing their share. Headed "Isn't It Romantic?" the feature offered readers' suggestions for "getting your husband to help." One "makes her husband's favorite dish when he has done half the chores on the to-do list she posts on the refrigerator." Another leaves "notes with instructions and 'love lines' on the refrigerator, doors, mirrors, the play yard, and the shower curtain." And then there is Alicia Puckett of Fort Collins, Colorado, who presented her husband with flowers before broaching the subject of shared housework. They agreed on "a 50-50 split," but so that his "enthusiasm wouldn't wane, two weeks later Alicia gave him a coupon book she created, for massages and candlelit bubble baths. 'My husband has never been so willing to help,' she reports."

THE LAWN VS. THE LAUNDRY

The tasks of choice for men—minor household repairs, mowing the lawn, shoveling snow, or taking out the trash—have some interesting characteristics in common. Besides being more traditionally male, all are more discretionary in terms of when they are done and what, if anything, they are done in combination with. These are also the kind of single-focus goal-satisfying tasks that men prefer. That anyone prefers, as it turns out.

And this is why housework is no small matter. Over and over again it has been shown that the degree of satisfaction or stress from work—paid or unpaid—is directly related to the control the worker has over getting the job done. Triumphing over a leaky faucet or sitting high up on a lawn mower for an hour of pleasant privacy amidst fresh scents of new-mown grass with a clear goal in sight is the antithesis of picking up dirty socks, sopping up baby spills, and emptying the dish-washer, in varying combinations, a zillion times a day. House-hold tasks are among the most low-control and high stress, right up there with assembly-line work and air traffic control. It is the stress of the job, compounded by the drone of the Dreaded Tape, not the minutes spent that takes a toll.

"At first glance, it might seem that for a man, getting out of these jobs is a good deal, since it means they'll escape a lot of stress," write psychologist Rosalind C. Barnett and jour-nalist Caryl Rivers in *She Works/He Works*. "But if this means their partner does it all, they will be living with a woman who's stressed-out, resentful, and angry. That's hardly the prescription for a happy marriage," or, since stress is the most common turnoff, a sex life.

Surprisingly, there may be something to be learned about stress reduction from the way men relate to housework.

For one thing, their standards are typically more flexible. As Philip puts it, "Only if I'm pushed in the heat of argument do I mention something like 'The clothes might have been put away today.' But routinely, I'm perfectly willing to accept the fact that she does what she's capable of doing during the day, and if it means I don't have every little thing in every room just right, I live with it. It just really doesn't bother me. My life is pretty good as it is, and if it doesn't get done, I can live with that."

Some of Philip's equanimity may be attributed to a general lack of experience with all that is involved short of getting "every little thing in every room just right." "If men cannot see the tasks," sociologist Polly Fassinger observes in an essay in *Men, Work, and Family,* "they are unable to take part in them." By interviewing divorced couples she was able to confirm that only when men have to set up house on their own, do they become fully aware of women's "invisible" work—"the logistics and routines of family care."

Robert's education came during the year he was an at-home parent. "Until I was home with my daughter, I didn't realize how much disorder bothers me. She loves to go around and pull all the books out of the bookshelf. If I've cleaned up her toy kitchen stuff and put everything back and she comes down five minutes later and trashes the thing again, that does bug me a lot." His frustration sounds familiar. "After dealing with that for five or six months, you kind of crave getting away from that and it has nothing to do with not loving your kid or anything. It just has to do with keeping your sense of order and your sanity."

The lesson for the woman who wants to promote a mother's helper is that she can talk until she is blue in the face, but unless she can get out of the way and let him experience the tide rising around his knees, nothing will happen.

Daniel found that housework came into his consciousness in a less cataclysmic way, once he was focusing on his family. "Before the baby was born, Penny had been going along with the assumption that the child care would be along the same lines as the housework—we'd talked a lot about how I should be doing 50 percent, but she ended up doing about 75 percent. Now I take care of Ingrid as much or more than Penny. And that has affected the housework. I think we're a lot closer to parity because it's just sort of gotten me into a very different state of mind. Before—I've always tended to get very wrapped up in my work and when I'm home my mind is still on the work and I don't really get focused on what I'm doing. So I'm pretty oblivious about the housework. Now with Ingrid, when I get home, she just kind of brings me down to earth a whole lot more. And I get a lot more focused on just feeding her, taking care of her, and then cleaning up after all of that. It comes a lot more naturally now."

What Daniel's experience demonstrates is that in an integrated life there is no dichotomy between stepping up to parenthood and stepping down to cleaning up after other people; it is all part of a natural process.

"DADDY'S RULES"

Fassinger's research has some disconcerting implications for women. We may have to be prepared to deal with—and even learn from—"Daddy's Rules." For one thing, men don't personalize the process. They maintain a healthy disconnect between themselves and what needs to be done. "Fathers were much more likely than mothers to feel that housekeeping was not a parental responsibility," writes Fassinger. Therefore, they were much more inclined to get the kids involved and insist that "housework was a family chore." As a result, when they asked for help from their children they would tell them that it is "not my job"; a mother is more inclined to ask for help because she "needs" it.

Robert is the main meal man because he gets home first. "Mealtime is always a source of tension and frustration," he says. But, he adds, "I don't personalize making dinner." The scene is familiar: "No matter what time of day it is, you're always gearing towards bedtime, and anything that holds up dinner then holds up the rest of the works. I want to be able to make dinner, have my three-year-old eat it, sitting at the table, not running around, and have it be over with."

Despite the pressure, he keeps an emotional distance from the process. "It's not like, 'I slaved over the stove.' It's more, 'We asked you what you wanted. You told us what you wanted. Now you won't eat it.' That's very frustrating." Then, with a sigh, he adds, "You don't want to just make grilled cheese every night."

Fassinger made another important discovery about housework. While the divorced men she interviewed found running a home hard to do on their own, their ex-wives found just the opposite. "Some mothers felt less stressed about the upkeep of their home," she writes, "because they no longer were frustrated by their spouse's participation (or lack thereof).... Their husband's delinquent or irresponsible behavior with regard to household chores had caused considerable tension." In other words, the women were experiencing some relief from a major item on the Dreaded Tape—or what Fassinger describes as "the component of family care that involves motivating or nurturing those who work with you." When women say, "It's easier to do it myself," they mean it's easier to do it than to negotiate and nag, but in the long run it is not easier to live with the smoldering resentment that builds up while doing it alone.

THE SAME JOB—VERY DIFFERENT REACTIONS

There is an appealing simplicity to one man's rule of thumb: As he told Gerson, "If we both have bad days, then whoever had the better day takes care of [our daughter]." The same goes for housework. "One thing I learned: you can't take domestic jobs and say, 'You do this, and I do that.'... I don't think that's right....You do it together. If she's too tired, then I do it; and if I'm too tired then she'll do it."

If, that is, they can get past trying to agree on which of them is "too tired."

Nick and Martha have a pretty low-stress approach to household tasks. "You know how jobs fall out, probably half-sexist and half-habit," Nick begins. "She does vacation planning. I do the car. I even own the car. She wasn't there, so I just signed it myself. Let's see, what else is there? There's housework... she'd probably say she does a little more of, but I do a pretty good amount. I do laundry and bring it upstairs; she puts it away."

Alan and Catherine have a similar understanding. "We didn't sit down and make up a list to make sure that we were exactly doing the same amount of stuff, but we were both pretty satisfied that it was evenly shared. The grocery shopping, she would do. The cleaning the bathrooms, I would do. The cutting the grass, washing the windows, I would do. The laundry's interesting. She does the wash; I do the ironing."

When they decided that one of them would be home with the kids until all three were in grade school and Alan's was the salary that could carry the family, they found another route to equity. "I think the cooking probably accounts for at least

50 percent of the household stuff, and she's definitely taken on major responsibility for that. But now we make sure that we go out for dinner a couple of times a week, with the kids usually. Once or twice a month we'll get a baby-sitter or the grandparents will come and visit while we go out. So we're pretty careful about making sure we do that."

They also took into account Catherine's need to stay connected with her work. "She's a registered nurse and volunteers at the local hospital and she substitutes whenever the elementary school nurse can't come in," Alan explains. On those days he makes it his business to be there when the kids get home. "In nursing, the technologies and medications and therapies are changing so quickly that it's important to stay current. And so she's doing that. But," he adds, "she'd rather be working."

When Philip, who experiences a great deal more conflict with his wife over housework, suggested an approach to the laundry that was similar to the one that worked for Alan and Nick, all hell broke loose. Philip was bewildered, because he thought the issue was laundry, when it was really the Dreaded Tape. "The other day I said to Helen, 'I understand how you feel about doing the laundry, I know you don't want to fold the clothes, I know you don't want to put the clothes away, it's not what you're living your life to do. If you will simply buy a laundry basket, take the clothes out of the dryer, dump them in the laundry basket, put them upstairs in the bedroom, I will personally fold them all and put them away.' Her answer was, "Well, I'm doing all the finances in the house, you can do *all* the laundry. Laundry is not me.'"

Women could take a cue from men on this one, to break "the connection between housework and their self-esteem" that Fassinger has observed. For their part, men need to *make* a connection, become attuned to the distinction between "doing and being responsible for a job." Ultimately, though, since "men and women define their responsibilities for housework differently," both have to understand that an equal division of tasks will not create equity. Instead, "behavioral equality may accompany distinctly different perceptions and motivations of men and women." In other words, in the end, it's not how equitable the division of labor is, but how fair it *feels*.

CHAPTER SEVEN

THE LEARNING CURVE

One of my first lessons was to accept the fact that all babies cry. Most men, myself included, like to be in control of their emotions and surroundings at all times, and a crying baby tends to quickly erode feelings of mastery. It took some time, but after a while I figured out the meanings of most of Kyle's wails.

—Lee Beadling, *American Baby*, June 1994

MANY YEARS AGO a young woman stood up after a lecture on finding independence and equality and told the audience about how she managed to break out of the only-mom-can-nurture mode. What she did was take a trip by herself one month after her baby was born, leaving her husband to cope alone for two weeks. "When I got home," she announced triumphantly, "they had bonded!" Most of the audience gasped; the rest cheered. The gaspers were horrified at the idea of walking out on her baby and leaving him in the clumsy hands of a man, albeit his father. They were also appalled that she had relinquished/abandoned her role/power. The cheer-ers—and there were many fewer of them—were impressed both by the courage it took to walk away from being indis-pensable, from taking on the mystique of the maternal role, and by the outcome: the father had been roped into equal parenting. The assumption was that he wasn't willing, that he needed to be trapped.

To both groups, though, it sounded like a cold and calcu-lating way of trying to break the mold. In an effort to clarify things, she explained that she and her husband had been very anxious to share parenting and for that reason had even decided against breast-feeding so that they could both feed their newborn. When they got home from the hospital, though, while both were panicky at their inexperience, she very quickly moved into high learning gear, while her hus-band fell easily into a backup stance. The aura of maternal mystery was gathering around her with her growing sense of confidence. She soon realized that if she was going to make room for her husband to assimilate the expertise she was soaking up, she would have to give him the opportunity to learn under the same circumstances: total immersion.

As the women explored their reactions, one remarked that the story reflected a far greater degree of trust and re-spect for the husband than many of them would bestow on their own partners. Others wondered if they would be willing to let go of the power and prestige and pleasure that come with being the guiding light in the family. Then another voice entered the conversation. "You know," she said, "what strikes me is the trust and respect she is showing her baby. She seems to know that she can count on the baby to make clear to his father what is needed in the same way as he communicated to his mother. What a gift to the whole family," she added thoughtfully, "to bind them together, right from the start, into a circle of trust, love, and communication!"

She was recognizing what most mothers don't often acknowledge to themselves, that the will to bond and empathize is awakened by the total dependency of an infant.

Indeed, the pattern of general and aide-de-camp sets in very early, about the same time as the connections between parent and infant begin to form. I was reminded of the runaway-mother story when, in the course of a long conversation with Carl, the basketball player turned human resources manager, I became aware of how quickly he had moved into second position. He spoke with joy and wonder about how his baby, born seven months earlier, had changed his life and dramatically rearranged his priorities. "I know that I'm not going to be a millionaire," he said. "But I also know that I'll be able to see my son and be a part of his life. I want to be home every day at six o'clock. Or at least have control enough over my schedule to determine when I'm not going to be." He was a little tired just then, he added, because the baby had been sick the previous weekend. He went on to describe how he and his wife had struggled with the decision of whether or not to call the doctor. "When I get home, I see him crying; I know he's upset, but I'm not sensitized to it, because she's been hearing it or seeing it all day," Carl began; still he recommended a wait-and-see stance, but his wife prevailed on him to place the call. "My wife starts giving me tips on what to say on the phone. So I say, 'Why don't you talk to the doctor,' but she gives me the standard fare: 'I want you to handle this, but I want to tell you how to handle it.'"

The pediatrician told them to bring the baby in and found a serious ear infection. "From then on," conceded Carl with a sigh, "I can never say, 'No, I don't think we should call the doctor,' because from then on she's always right."

He sounded chagrined at his failure of instinct and grateful that wiser heads (his wife, the General's) had prevailed. He voiced the by-now-familiar admiration for his wife's ability to deal with the baby. A question I had not asked the other fathers occurred to me: How long, I asked him, would be the limit of time he could spend alone with the baby? "Twenty minutes!" he blurted out. "Twenty minutes before total panic would set in."

Seven months into parenting and seven months into a major shift of his work attitude and his schedule, and Carl is already way behind in the basic skills of meeting his baby's needs. He is also losing opportunities to find his own style of response, which may well be very different from his wife's nurturing. At this rate, it will be harder and harder for him to tune in to the nuances of his child's emotional and physical needs, and he will be well on the way to disqualifying himself from fulfilling the one overarching need, according to Carol Gilligan, that every child has. All children need "someone who tracks them emotionally" as they pass through all the difficult stages of self-discovery and engagement with the world.

Parenting is a learning process for all concerned. And everyone changes with every station of the cross, from infancy through adolescence. It simply isn't possible to go with the flow if you aren't in the water, too.

That is probably the best argument for parental leave: it's not that newborns need so much special care, but that the parent who doesn't get into the game then will have a harder time later picking up the language, the codes, the rituals. (In fact, if all things were equal, many parents would say that an equally important time for parental leave is when the kids are adolescents and you really need to be on the scene to pick up clues about what is going on.)

BIOLOGY AND DESTINY

Like most human relationships, though, wishing doesn't always make it so. As ardently as mothers and fathers may plight their troth to coparenting, each brings a complex personal and

171

cultural history to what is already a complex and unequal biological process. A well-worn feminist put-down of job discrimination points out that the only jobs with bona fide gender requirements are "wet nurse and sperm donor." While those are absurdly marginal professions, what they imply in the dynamic of even the most egalitarian family is no joke. As Dorothy Dinnerstein insists, the sperm donor's freedom to walk away from his progeny seconds after the act and the nursing mother's bond with her progeny create a chasm in parenting that is full of demons.

Women don't have to look very far for evidence of men who have neglected their children. Most mothers have what-iffed being left in the lurch. Men may be less conscious of how they can be shut out until they are face-to-face with their nursing offspring. Many of the men I talked to seemed genuinely bewildered and disappointed when they realized that, as one put it, from the point of view of his newborn son, his wife "had the goods."

Conrad was more expansive. "The feeling sets in very, very quickly that the principle of wanting to play an equal role is completely undeliverable in practice because you don't have breasts and you don't have milk and you don't have the things your baby wants. . . . You wake up in the middle of the night and you have all this kind of goodwill and you want to play your full part and you pick up the baby and say, 'You go back to sleep, sweetheart, I'll take the baby this time,' and you go into the other room and the baby goes, 'Waa, waa, waa, waa' and you put up with it for ten minutes and you get very exasperated and you transfer your exasperation pretty quickly onto the baby and you go back and say, 'I tried, but he wants you.' . . . I remember fighting with some stuff in those early days about feeling rejected by the kid. . . . To want to be super close to an infant is very hard, because it's based on nothing but need—there's the smiling and the playing, of course, and all that stuff which was delicious and wonderful, but a lot of the time with an infant, where the needs are pre-verbal, the mother is just objectively in a much better place to supply those needs. I used to feel miffed and jealous some-times; I'm sure I used to express that."

This sense of uselessness and resentment was echoed by many other fathers, who conceded that their behavior may have contributed to uncertainty on their wives' part about their commitment to the job, especially when the going gets rough—which typically happens right away.

Paul had been so eager for fatherhood that he kept a journal throughout his wife's pregnancy reviewing his fears and expectations in minute detail. Then Jacob arrived.

"And *froom* it was all out the window. The first eight weeks were really hard. The biggest surprise was that he needed his mother more than me. And I got really jealous; I had mother envy. Beth was breast-feeding, and I think I wanted to do too much and we would be practically elbowing

173

each other for who's going to do the work. I could change him, but if he was crying, the only one who could really placate him was Beth, so I was sort of just hanging around.

"As a friend of ours, who is also a father, said, 'The first few weeks, when it's just running around and cleaning up, it's like being a janitor in a whorehouse.' You're kind of cleaning up the slop and running errands," he explained. "I was shocked at how difficult it was; I began to worry that I'd never love him as much as I love my cat."

Natalie Angier, in her book *Woman, An Intimate Geography*, explains what is lost to the "janitor in the whorehouse"—a visceral connection with a newborn. "How often . . . does the average father sit and rock his baby against his naked breast? Not often enough, and not nearly as often as the average mother does. Mothers tend to monopolize their babies. . . . Too often a father's contact with his baby is restricted to those times when the mother is tired and wants a break, and so it becomes a chore and a duty to him rather than a rite. He keeps his shirt on. He's buttoned up. The nerve endings of his flesh detect the baby's frequency only faintly."

Stan, a single father, recalls the advice of his pediatrician. "Instead of bathing the baby in the tub, he told me, take him in the shower with you. That way you will make skin contact more often and more intimately." Stan was eligible for this advice only because he was like the understudy forced to go on when the star couldn't make it. The pediatrician probably wouldn't have said the same thing to a father who came in with his wife and baby and surely wouldn't have thought bonding advice for the mother was necessary. Other men could learn plenty from Stan and the over one and a half million other single fathers: There is nothing mysterious about bonding, and even the "janitor" can move up.

"INSTINCT"

Beyond and beneath and all around the biological barriers that confront new fathers is the swirl of everything else that falls under the umbrella of "instinct." What part of parenting as we know it can be taught, what part can be learned, and what parts will be modified by men are questions that will undoubtedly remain unanswered for this generation of fathers. They will just muddle through as best they can.

Virtually all those I talked to admitted that they weren't total parental partners, though a handful felt they had gotten pretty close. None achieved the totality of "parental involvement" calibrated by Michael Lamb, an expert on child development. He divides the definition of involvement into three parts: "engagement"—one-on-one time with the child, commonly known as "quality time"; "accessibility"—where the parent is doing something else but is ready to respond to the child if necessary (which parent is more likely to be interrupted during the meal by the constant demands of "Cut up my meat," "Pour my soda," "Oops, I spilled...."?); and "responsibility"—being accountable for the child's welfare, the Dreaded Tape, in other words. Lamb found that in families where both parents worked outside the home, fathers spent about one-third as much time as mothers did being engaged, two-thirds as much time being accessible, and a minimal amount of time being responsible.

While this generation of fathers isn't approaching the totality of maternal parenting, they are learning a lot—and getting a lot in return. As James recalls, he didn't know what he "knew" until he felt it. "The second day Markie was home, I was dressing him and talking to him. And my wife said, 'What are you talking to the kid for?' And I said, 'If you were him, what would you want? I'm explaining to him about the two shirtsleeves and two armholes and one head hole. I'm telling him stuff because this is how I want this relationship to be. It's just coming out of me.... This is the way it has to be."

Now, eight years and a second son later, he is wiser but no less emotional. "I cannot believe the incredible amount of work this is. I can't believe that uncategorized, unmeasurable, incredible pleasure that it's giving me. They are just tremendous, clear pools of nectar for me and I can't get enough."

Enthusiasts like James will make it easier for men like Carter to find models for the kind of fatherhood they "instinctively" want to experience. "You look at the culture and you look at the macho types and you look at the feminist male types and you say, 'Is there an alternative between the Clint Eastwoods and the Alan Aldas?'" Carter found one in—of all places—Bill Murray's character in the movie *Ghostbusters*. "It's kind of a nonchalant thing," he explains, that works for him and his daughter. "I think Jessica has prospered by having a father who asks certain goofy questions and who plays games, who makes up words, much in the way that Bill Murray does with Sigourney Weaver." He also goes for the *Ghostbusters* look. "The slovenliness of Bill Murray's presentation is appealing." It conveys the message that a father doesn't have to be the tough and austere figure Carter's own father was, that he can also be "really playful and grunged up . . . relaxed and enjoying the moment and enjoying the kid." The payoff? "Jessica has a kind of great little grin that she gives when she's saying something that's a tease."

Other men gain confidence and commitment with each child. Robert, whose second daughter, Carrie, was born eight months ago, cherishes the rituals of parenting. "At bedtime, Karin and I switch off, one of us usually gives our four-year-old a bath and the other one gets her to sleep. And the baby still runs on a baby clock. Karin is still nursing her, though I do some bottles during the day. I'll feed her some, too—she's eating food—and give her a bottle here and there. I always liked when Lily was a baby, just putting her to sleep at night; we would switch off giving her a bottle at the end of the evening. It was just a very nice time, even if it took a while to get her to sleep. I imagine we'll begin to swap off in a couple of months, when breast-feeding is over. Neither of us wants to give up being the last one that she sees when she goes to sleep at night."

What makes it particularly hard for men to follow their nurturing instincts is that many of those instincts have been bred out of them as they grew up. As Michael Kimmel and Michael Messner point out in their book *Men's Lives,* "the important fact of men's lives is not that they are biological males, but that they become men. Our sex may be male, but our identity as men is developed through a complex process of interaction with the culture."

Instinctive response requires a kind of fluency between knowledge and feeling that women seem more adept at and are certainly more rewarded for; men have not been trained to feel very comfortable listening to their emotions. In fact, they are traditionally directed toward stifling feelings of any kind and controlling expressions of pain, fear, not knowing what to do.

Geoffrey Canada, author of *Reaching Up for Manhood,* who grew up in a rough New York City neighborhood, voices one especially poignant regret—that he once praised a ten-year-old for not crying after a painful injury. "I have come to see that in teaching boys to deny their own pain we inadvertently teach them to deny the pain of others."

And conversely—though this happens much less often—when a father is tuned in to his child's emotional needs, he can find himself ministering to his own as well. A man interviewed by Scott Coltrane in *Family Man* characterizes himself as "very shy" and sees the same quality in his kids. "They say, 'Daddy, would you go up to Sarah's door?' and I feel embarrassed to go up to Sarah's door too, but I'm trying to get my kid to understand how to deal with people, so I do it. It's been very instructive for me, I mean I've learned a lot, not just in raising kids, but about myself, by having kids."

The contemporary father, even the rebel, has been well indoctrinated in classic masculinity and fatherhood, and no matter how much he wants to chart a different course, that is the one he knows best. In order to overcome that history, he has to reactivate skills, particularly emotional skills, he unlearned growing up. Can those skills be taught? Ronald F. Levant, a psychologist at Boston University, has developed an eight-week course for fathers who are not satisfied with the way they are connecting to their kids. The course focuses on helping men pay attention to their emotions (including rage and frustration—two emotions common to both parents and children), deal with their fear of intimacy, and learn simple communications skills. Levant's curriculum also includes nutrition and child development and hygiene, but that's the easy stuff.

Designed to "fit men's traditional learning styles and to help men develop certain psychological skills that many men do not ordinarily acquire because of the male socialization process," the course teaches communications skills and child management. It incorporates role-playing and videotaping techniques into a format that is, according to Levant, male-friendly; the program is described to prospective students as "educational" and an "opportunity to develop skills," along the lines of a golf or tennis clinic, and the video equipment that is in the meeting room is, in addition to being functional, thought to be the kind of "hardware...which may provide a feeling of familiarity given men's traditional relationship to machinery."

The videos of role-playing exercises can be pretty shocking to the participants; one saw himself towering over the "child" he was talking to, another was taken aback to see himself talking from behind a newspaper. The group realized that both forms of "talking" had very little to do with communicating. The men work on listening to members of their family and looking for nonverbal clues—like their own towering over or hiding behind—that may say more than words.

As they move through the exercises, the men discover that they don't even have the words to acknowledge, let alone describe to someone else, what they are feeling. Levant encourages group members to keep logs of their emotions over a period of time and gives them lists of words to use as they overcome what he calls "emotional numbness." Some of the words on his list are "abandoned" and "amused," "defeated" and "delighted," "petrified" and "proud," "rejected" and "remorseful," "trapped" and "tender."

Little by little the fathers in Levant's course become aware of the range of emotions that they had been hiding under the umbrella of "I'm tired" or behind the truncheon of anger. As they chart the terra incognita of the emotional landscape, the men find themselves increasingly empathic and increasingly able to give others in their families the emotional nutrition they crave. They also begin to learn who their children are, that children have their own internal frame of reference, that they often express their feelings through action, that they have minds of their own.

One of Levant's "students" was transformed by what he discovered once he began paying real attention to his daughter: "I was accustomed to doing things at my pace, and the first thing I learned is that you can't expect a four-year-old to come up to your speed. You have to slow down to hers, which was a rough adjustment at first. But, you know, a lot of wonderful stuff happens when you spend that kind of time with your kid. Like, my daughter and I got into this ritual where I'd wake her up, and then I'd sit with her before she got out of bed while she told me her dreams. It hadn't even occurred to me that she *had* dreams—that's how out of touch I was.... So we'd talk about her dreams. And then we'd do the bathroom routine, and all the while, she'd be chattering away about whatever came into her mind. And she'd be asking me questions like 'What makes water hot?' and 'Why does it get dark at night?' And then we'd pick out what she wanted to wear that day. I discovered that my daughter has definite tastes in clothes. She likes sweaters but she doesn't like blouses. She'll wear yellow, but she won't wear green because green is 'yukky.' It was like I was really starting to know her for the first time."

Steven Lewis, the author of *Zen and the Art of Father-hood*, didn't take a course in fathering, unless you count raising seven children, but he learned the same lessons. He describes an experience that called upon all his empathy and understanding of his daughter's emotional universe. He was on his way to pick Addie up from kindergarten at the appointed time, 3:05, but he got stuck in traffic. When, at 3:25, he bounded up the steps of the now-deserted school building, he rushed past the teacher and down the hall toward his five-year-old. She raced toward him and for a moment he thought it was all no big deal, a disappointment that could be cured by a compensatory ice-cream cone, but then he realized she was sobbing in his arms. Then she was pounding his chest; that was when he got the message: "I realized just how afraid she had been, how elated she had been to see me, how furious and frustrated she had felt to be forgotten, and how all that was happening at the same time—laughing, crying, hitting—all in equal measure."

He was shocked that Addie was breaking the family taboo against ever hitting a parent. Steven and his wife had made this rule an especially inviolate one. They didn't like the idea of encouraging "little pugilists" with "a frightfully exaggerated sense of their own power."

But this time, he knew—with a visceral certitude—was different. "That afternoon I allowed Addie to pound my aching chest while I gathered her up in my arms and held her close to my heart until she calmed down." He saw how the experience looked to her. "No matter how silly or inconsequential it may seem to the adult mind, I knew that Addie was not old enough or wise enough to understand about chronically late parents. The hurt she felt went all the way down to the dark core of her easily frustrated being—and cried out for the kinds of balance that only hitting your daddy could satisfy. Sometimes you just have to balance the ledger, even if it is wrong."

No nurturing mother could have put it better.

An even wider pattern of ripples emanating from parenting skills reached daughter/wife/mother/psychologist Barbara Katz Rothman. "I remember my own awkwardness providing 'nursing' care to my mother during an illness of hers in my adolescence," she wrote in *Reclaiming Motherhood*. "I compare that with the competence with which I can now provide such care. And I particularly remember my husband's awkwardness providing such care to me before our first child, and the skill and ease with which he does it now. Nursing me through my first labor, he was infinitely well meaning. Nursing me through my second, he knew what he was doing. He had been nurturing for seven years, years of nursing earaches, bellyaches, changing diapers, calming night terrors, holding pans for vomit, taking out splinters, washing bloody wounds. He had grown accustomed to the sheer physicality of the body, the sights and sounds and smells. More essentially, what I showed him in my pain and my fear was not foreign—he saw the baby, the child in me, not the one I was birthing, but the one I myself am, and he nursed it. Now *that* is a man to enter old age with."

AMBIVALENCE

"Society sends men two messages," says psychologist Jerrold Lee Shapiro. "The first is, We want you to be involved, but you'll be an inadequate mother. The second is, You're invited into the birthing room and into the nurturing process—but we don't want all of you. We only want your support. We're not really ready as a culture to accept men's fears, their anger or their sadness. This is the stuff that makes men crazy." Furthermore, Shapiro worries, "If you become Mr. Mom, the family has a mother and an assistant mother. That isn't what good fathers are doing today."

What exactly *are* good fathers doing today? No one seems sure. The ambivalence among both men and women that shows up in poll after poll about whether mothers should work outside the home (40 percent think not, according to a 1997 Families and Work Institute national "Study on the Changing Work Force") or whether mothers are more nurturing is as much about familying fathers as working mothers.

When asked, 93 percent of men and women told the *Washington Post* that ideally "Everything about the care of children should be shared equally by both parents." But precisely what would that mean? Should involved fatherhood be more like motherhood? And if not, how should it be?

A tantalizing finding comes from Ellen Galinsky's study of children of working parents. She compared how parents graded themselves with how their kids graded them and came up with some challenging discrepancies, including this one: While fathers gave themselves lower marks than mothers gave themselves on such items as "Being there for your child," "Knowing what is really going on in your child's life," and "Controlling your temper," the fathers' self-evaluations were closer to their kids' ratings of them than the mothers' were. Why is this? Galinsky asks. "Do mothers tie their identity and self-esteem more closely to how good a parent they are? Perhaps mothers need to see themselves as competent? Are fathers more realistic about what they are good at and what they aren't?"

Right from the start there are no answers, only questions and the fear of the unknown.

Those questions and fears are likely to be compounded, not resolved, by the first few months of family life. Drs. Phil and Carolyn Cowan, who studied new parents in 1997, were "amazed" to discover "how little time fathers allowed themselves for uncertainty" and for learning by the standard method of trial and error, and "how quickly mothers stepped in if father or baby looked uneasy." They were less astonished to discover that the more incompetent the fathers felt, the more they withdrew.

THE FEAR FACTOR—PAUL

Paul is the fellow who started a journal as soon as he knew he was going to be a father, so by the time Jacob was born he had had many conversations with himself about the new role. When I met with him again, five-month-old Jacob was playing on the floor. In a while he got cranky and Paul soothed him; then Jacob needed to be changed. "Honey, don't eat your diaper. This has got to go on you," Paul cooed. "It's not very tasty." That relaxed good humor was a hard-won state of mind.

"At first, I had this huge fear that a huge change was coming," he recalls, "and I didn't know if I could handle it. I thought he would just be a kind of blob. I couldn't see the totality of the child's development. All I saw was, Oh my god, he's little and he's crying, he's crying, he doesn't recognize me, all he wants is his mother, and it's always going to be that way. And it's going to be exhausting and complete turmoil." Then there were the immediate indignities. "When I changed him I was like, 'Oh my god, this smells.' And I got kind of panicky—like, am I going to be able to handle this? Now," he adds, "I just don't breathe out of my nose."

As a freelancer, Paul was able to organize his time to be home a lot right after Jacob was born. After three weeks, he kind of flipped out. "I had a dream where I killed him," he says, shamefacedly aware of the impact of his words, although the fantasy is more common among young parents, men *and* women, than they know. "I dreamed I electrocuted him on the train tracks. Then he's dead and I'm thinking, I shouldn't have done that. I think I feel bad about this. We told everybody we had this baby and I was kind of looking forward to having him and . . . god. I really felt regretful in the dream. And then I realized maybe I should have given him another chance."

When he awoke, he was "so happy it was a dream—that feeling of ultimate relief." Paul's dream came at a turning point in his relationship with Jacob, but not, it turns out, in terms of his ambivalence. "Coincidentally, the next day Beth first pumped and I gave him his bottle; he took it right away and just really opened up for a lot more of a bond with him."

The same could not be said about Paul's relationship with Beth. "We were fighting; we weren't intimate. We were like focusing on the baby, not each other, and we were getting very tense and estranged. Beth was feeling isolated at home and I'd come home emotionally remote—I can get snappy and sarcastic. We had a big blowup and kind of aired all our grievances, and things got better."

The grievances were a litany of mixed messages, as Paul tells it. "I think I was giving schizophrenic signals. On the one hand, I'm saying I want to get the hell out of the house and get back to work because I feel like I'll never get back to work if I don't go. On the other hand, I want to be the mother." And there was something else: "I think I was getting mad at her because I felt that she was micromanaging me with Jacob, like standing over my shoulder. And I would get really defensive and like, 'Why are you telling me how to do it. You don't trust me? You don't have confidence in me?'

"I remember bathing him, and she said, 'You've got to be calmer when you give him a bath at night, because he's got to go to sleep and he needs to calm down.' And I thought I was just playing—maybe I would kind of hold him over my head and she didn't like it at that time of day—and I got mad at her. She was probably right, but I just wanted to have a relationship with him."

Beth tried to convince him that her pointers were not meant as criticism. "'I'm not criticizing,' she said; 'I'm just trying to help.' And I said, 'Well, that may be true, but I get very sensitive to criticism and you have to let me do it *my* way as long as it's not 180 degrees different from the way *you* would do it. There's got to be variations and there could be the way Mommy acts and the way Daddy acts, but if they're in concert with each other, that's OK.'"

The ambivalence wasn't only on his part, he thinks. "I got mad that she didn't pump enough at first. So I couldn't do many bottles. She had some issues about it—she didn't like this machine sucking her milk out, taking food out of her body, and she felt kind of proprietary about feeding him."

Now that he and Beth are through that first rough spot, Paul has a better idea of what being a family is about. "Jacob has brought out a good empathetic side of me, and I think I've become much more emotionally accessible. I think he's been a really good influence on me spiritually. I used to be much more callous."

Paul has a rare opportunity to compare how he has come

through the early trials with other new fathers. "Beth is in this mommies group at the Y and sometimes the fathers will get together, too," and Paul is witness to tensions that probably wouldn't emerge outside the privacy of the couples' several homes. "A lot of those fathers are totally terrified about their kids. And the wives are really resentful that the fathers aren't more involved, and it's really sad," he says.

"One husband is like, 'Well, you wanted to have him and I didn't' and he refuses to do anything with the kid. Some are like, 'Well, he doesn't really like me, he likes his mother. . . .' All of these guys are like 'Well, I'll play ball with him when he gets older.' But this is an important time now, too, and there's more to it than playing ball."

With the perspective of a survivor, he concludes, "I think a lot of men start out scared. I know I was. It's like we say to ourselves, 'Oh, I'm scared; this is women's work. I don't want to deal with it. So I'll just withdraw.' Which is the male way of handling things. If someone had to step up to the plate, he'd probably do it, but if the mother is available, it's easy for the father to defer or withdraw."

STARTING EARLY

In fact, all the men I met who did "step up to the plate" felt they had to push their way into the lineup—or be pushed.

Some, like Clint, a factory worker from Wyoming, who was out of a job, were pushed by circumstances. Others, like Andrew whose wife worked longer hours than he, had to cope for a period of time every day on their own, making mistakes, doing it their way, without anyone looking over their shoulders. Yet others, like Daniel, had to put their efforts where their words were. Most, like Carl, took it slowly. In all cases, though, the only way was total immersion, whether only twenty minutes at the start or two weeks.

Although Carl has organized his work life to be home at six, he is the classic what-do-I-do-now new father. When we first spoke, he confessed that more than twenty minutes alone with his baby set off a panic attack. A few months later he looked back on those days with a bit more confidence. "My wife would leave the room and I'd be like, 'Where are you going?' Or she would leave the house, and I'd be like, 'What time are you going to be back? So I can watch the clock to make sure that you're back in time. Because I can only keep him at bay for about twenty minutes and after that I'm at his mercy.' The first time she went to the doctor—she was gone for like forty-five minutes, I was looking out the window. The second time she was gone, I didn't even notice she was gone. So far my record is two hours. My guess is that half a day is the most I'd be able to do without him going nuts and me, too." But Carl is also beginning to take some pride in his performance: "I took him to the store with me one time, which was a miraculous moment. He cried the whole way there and the whole way back, but he was still with *me*!"

WORKING AT IT—ANDREW

As is his wont, Andrew, the easy-going surgeon, has a very methodical view of the learning process: "I consider myself to be a very good father and I love my children, who are now four and seven, but when they're zero to six months, as a father, you have very, very little connection with that child other than what you try to fabricate. If you don't make the effort early on and you let it kind of slip by, it's lost and there's no question about it. I look at my brother who I love dearly, we're very close, but I don't think he's ever changed his daughter's diaper and she's now a year old. I think that that's both his fault and his wife's fault, but I think that he's lost a serious connection there."

Andrew escaped the same fate because he was on his own for a part of every day from the start. "When Annabel went back to work at six months, I was doing as many if not more of the diapers than she did, no question. I did a lot of the cooking; I did a lot of the wash or whatever needed to be done." Not that he didn't need a gentle nudge. "Annabel sort of forced me to do it in the beginning. I think that was the time when I really became an equal parent; I was able to change a diaper faster than anybody else and feed the kids and get them dinner and get them in a bath.

"My brother has never given his child a bath. To me that's unbelievable, because I was in the tub with them from the time they were little tiny things, holding them in the tub. I forced myself to create a bond; that's when you take on half of the parenting duties—truly take on half, not just the important decisions. You feel much more of a vested interest because you have established those ties."

He knows the tricks and the pitfalls. "It's easy to hand it off. Especially if the wife makes you feel inept, which I've seen—'Oh, he can't change a diaper,' laughing about it— that to me is ridiculous, stupid. I would be embarrassed to admit that my husband couldn't change a diaper, but that's accepted in our society. And it's also accepted for the man to say he's been working hard all week, and why shouldn't he be able to go off and play golf with his friends all day on Saturday and Sunday, and then go out at night with his wife because that's her time to spend with him?"

He has also come to see intangible ways in which one equal parent can be less equal than the other. "One thing I've noticed, and I don't know whether this is primordial, environmental, genetic, but I think Annabel feels a more palpable pain when she is away from the children than I do. I miss the boys so much when I'm away from them, but I know that I will see them. I guess the bottom line is, I've been raised to know that I have a job that I need to do. She feels more guilt and she feels more pain.

"It may be the environment in which she was raised; it may be her friends; it may be what she reads, it may be—there are so many environmental stimuli that it's probably hard to actually pinpoint it."

Then he zeroes in on what must feel like the highest validation of his efforts. Not total equality, but doing his share in a big way. "Annabel tells me—and I believe that this is true—that she feels a hundred percent better when I'm with the kids. Now, she feels probably 40 percent better when they're with our nanny because our nanny's great, but our nanny's not their parent. So she feels much more at ease and much better, and really all the guilt sort of goes away when I'm there with them."

CO-DIAPERING—DANIEL

Daniel, who is very new to the game, makes a similar point: "I think Penny finds it very, very reassuring that she can go away on her trips and feel confident that I'm going to take good care of Ingrid."

But in their case, Daniel had to push his way farther into the equation than Penny had been prepared for. He might not have done so if it weren't for a push he was given by the professional circumstances he found himself in—following his wife to a very prestigious academic assignment at the other end of the country from their New England home. "I'd had very competitive high-profile jobs," says Daniel, "and the move here was a huge professional setback for me. But I think it was only after coming to terms with all that, that I got to a place where I was ready to be a good father." Another reason may be that they are older; he is thirty-eight and Penny is forty-two.

"For medical reasons, we bottle-fed the baby, so from the beginning we were both interchangeable as far as Ingrid was concerned. Then, when she was about eight weeks old we started trading off taking Ingrid to work with us. I'd been reading in a lot of books that carrying the baby is very important for her sense of security, and that babies who are carried are a lot happier, don't cry as much. And that was certainly our experience. Once we started doing it, I loved the feel of having this baby right up next to me."

The surprise came when Penny had to go to a conference on the West Coast. "She had figured that we could try to do fifty-fifty when she was home but that when she had to travel, she'd have to take Ingrid with her and make daycare arrangements. Then, when she was talking about the arrangements she was making, I said, 'Wait a minute, what are you going to do? This can't be good for Ingrid to go off on this thing with you. Why shouldn't she stay with me?' I think it was very startling to Penny that I would be taking the initiative and saying, 'I want you to leave Ingrid with me, so I can take care of her.'"

Even with all the bottles and all the carrying around, Daniel found it "kind of scary being all on my own with the baby, but mostly it felt very natural." Surprisingly, it was harder for Penny to get used to the idea that, as Daniel put it, "she could really be confident that I'd be able to take good care of Ingrid and that this was how we were going to do things."

If there is any problem it is when, as the song goes, there's "something that must be done and it can only be done by one." "We're so competitive for Ingrid's attention," Daniel admits, "that we joke that she is probably the only baby for whom there have been plenty of times where when her diaper needs to be changed or she's throwing up and both parents are saying, 'No, give her to me, give her to me!'"

After twenty months, Daniel feels there is truly no "primary caregiver." In some measure this is Ingrid's doing as well as her parents'. "Ingrid has been enormously powerful at getting me much more focused on Ingrid when I'm taking care of her—sometimes I really get focused on just kind of crawling around the floor with her."

The payoff has been peace of mind. "We've invested so much into having a really intellectual and professional life, and so it is very important to us that we can really share Ingrid and then have our time when we go away and do our work. I think Ingrid responds equally to both of us as her primary caregiver. We take a lot of pride in that."

CLINT TAKES OVER

Clint didn't take up full-time parenting by choice, and he hadn't become a father that willingly, either, but he quickly found the whole package "kind of neat." He had been working double shifts in a lumber mill before he and his wife, Charlene, moved several states west to a town where she found a well-paid secretarial job and he didn't find work. So he spent six months at home with his two-year-old and three-year-old. The whole experience was a revelation. "Especially for someone who didn't want kids, it's really great to find out that they really want you and need you for everything," he says. "I baby-sat the kids and washed them and took care of everything. All of a sudden the roles changed because Mom would come home and the kids would need something and they wouldn't go to Mom, they'd come to Dad if they wanted their socks or their clothes, since I put them away in a different spot than Mom did. They actually like me cooking breakfast better than Mom. Mom gives them a piece of toast, and she's out the door. I cook them anything they want—scrambled eggs, French toast, waffles." Of course, he quickly picked up on the downside. "Twenty-four hours a day with kids gets on your nerves sometimes. They have their moments."

Now even though Clint's back to work, things have changed. His wife is working, too, so her paycheck helps with the finances; that means he can stay connected to his role in the family. They have moved back to the town they left, and he has gotten a job at the lumber mill again, where, as low man on the totem pole, he is the on-call person. The call could come at any time of the day or night. But he's figured out how to maintain some control. "We got caller ID, so I know if they're calling me. If I don't answer the phone, I don't have to go in. So I can actually be here at home when I need to be."

BONDING IN MINUTE ONE—MARTIN

Martin was more possessed than pushed, possessed by a certainty that overcame him of what he had to do. He literally bullied his way into his son's first hours. He tells the story in a breathless narrative:

"As soon as the baby was born they said, 'OK, we have to take your baby to weigh him.' 'OK, I'm coming with him.' 'Oh no, you can't come with him.' 'Why can't I come with him?' And I said, 'Not only that, I'm not letting go of my kid.' 'No, New York State law says that it has to be rolled in this special little space pod.'

"So at two in the morning, I'm padding down the hall; I have my chest on the little guy, because I'm thinking, How does *he* know, if I leave, if I'm ever gonna come back?

"So we get to the neonatal unit and they start to treat the kid like he's part of a factory. They're like swabbing him and wiping him and sticking him here and sticking him there. Then they weigh him. And then they take the diaper off and he has that—what's the word for it?—the meconium. The first poop. Which is this big black piece of goo. And I said, 'Excuse me. How much does that thing weigh?' And she said, 'I don't know; it's big, about a pound.' And I said, 'So my kid just lost a pound. Now, if I wasn't here, I'd be worrying for the next two weeks that my child hasn't regained birth weight. Why don't you weigh him after the meconium? I don't care if he's a pound less. I won't be bragging to everyone.'

"Then they start washing him and diapering him and swaddling him and they said, 'Why don't you go back to your room?' And I said, 'No, I'm not leaving my child's side. And that's that.' And they're laughing at me.

"And then I look around and there were twenty babies screaming—poor little kids. And I said, 'Where are their parents?' And the woman said, 'They're enjoying a well-deserved rest.' And I said, 'But these kids are having their first day on earth in misery—in bright lights, in a sterile room; why doesn't one of the parents—the father didn't have to work so hard, I mean I drove some and held her hand and I've got lots of energy.' The nurse said, 'Oh well, blah-blah I think the parents would rather be alone.'

"So I wait, and then I took my child back to the room, and we tried to put the baby in bed with my wife. Nope, not allowed to do that, you have to put him in this little cribby. So the minute they left, we put the kid in the bed and then *I* got in the bed.

"Then they found out I was in the bed, and I had to be very threatening. I said, 'Leave us alone, or you're gonna really regret it.' And they did.

"Another thing that bugged me in the hospital. They kept saying, 'Mother's name?' Her name is Stella. 'Child's name?' Aaron. And I was like 'Don't you have another question?' 'No, that'll be all.' I said, 'What about father's name?' And the woman actually said, 'How do we know you're the father?'

"What if the father's here? What if he's trying to be a good dad? Give him some encouragement here; let's try and encourage some family feeling here instead of making guys feel like they're some piece of meat."

BETTER LATE THAN NEVER—BRIAN

Brian was the slow starter who showed such patience with his teenage son; he has finally made himself a trusted part of seventeen-year-old Billy's life. And that entitled him to have the conversation he had been dreading since the day his son was born. "I had never sat down and discussed with him the circumstances under which Elizabeth and I got married. He's a smart kid and I'm sure he's figured it out somewhere along the way, but I knew sooner or later, I'd have to discuss it with him. I did that in the context of his girlfriend."

The conversation went from the general to the specific. "I said, 'I'm really concerned about teen pregnancy. Trust me, you don't want to be in a situation where your girlfriend is pregnant. I don't want to know if you are having sex.... I'm sure you figured it out by now, but you and I had never talked about it, and I just want to let you know that I faced—when I was young, not too much older than you are now—I was twenty—Mommy and I had ... we had to accelerate our marriage plans. We were going to get married and then Mommy was pregnant and we got married sooner than we otherwise would have. So I want to make sure you don't have that situation.'" That was it. Brian was drained, but looking back, he says, "I think it went pretty well."

One advantage that Brian thinks he has is that he is not so far removed from his son's age as many fathers are and can therefore call upon his own experience for understanding. (Experiences don't always mesh so compatibly. Psychologists have observed that "the father's progression through the developmental stages of adulthood often does not coincide neatly with the developmental stages of his children. For instance, middle-aged fathers undergoing a redefinition of their lives... might have adolescent children who are progressing through their own tumultuous identity crises.")

The fathers who do stick it out through adolescence reap a double reward. A famous forty-year study of 240 Boston fathers and sons found that good fathering led to adult success for the sons; less anticipated was the finding that good fathering also led to later success for the fathers. "Those fathers, having taken the time to negotiate this difficult passage, went on to enjoy better promotions in the workplace and to be involved in other important caregiving activities, such as being a coach, a union officer, or a civic leader. "That's the take-home: a man who can learn the skills necessary to guide a son through the teen years is ready for anything," summed up Michael Segell in *Esquire* magazine.

With his daughter, Anita, who is two years younger than Billy, Brian finds he can be more direct and not wait for an opening. "She's usually happy and giggly and goofy and in a good mood, so if something's bugging her, you know it. Then you have to chip away. You have to sit with her. 'What's wrong?' 'Nothing.' 'What's wrong?' 'Nothing.' 'Well, what's bothering you? How come you don't look happy?' I just bug her.... I'll sit down wherever she is and bug her until she finally breaks down and tells me."

With each encounter Brian has become more confident about trusting his instincts with his kids. "I'm very observant and very perceptive. But they don't know that. They'd be paranoid if they knew that I was watching, but I watch their every move and analyze it, and I watch for patterns," he confesses sotto voce. He has also incorporated a couple of lessons from his own growing up. "My father wasn't part of the rule-making process. He just let my mother make the rules on the ship. But my mother was overprotective: I had a stupid curfew; it was embarrassing and humiliating to have to be home at nine when my friends could stay out till eleven. I always felt the rules she made were based not on her judgment of my ability to handle situations, they were based on her fears. That was totally unfair. She was inflexible. I was not going to put my kids through that."

GETTING IT RIGHT

No parent can say he or she has it figured out, but in each of my conversations with fathers, there was a moment that sparked with the electricity of the real thing, a broken-in old shoe of an insight that can only be achieved by being there as your children happen.

Alan's moment came in a throwaway observation: "When the kids get sick, they come to whoever happens to be there. If we're both there, they usually come to me. I think it's because Mom's a nurse, and she gets very clinical with them. From the time they were young, she was very comforting and nurturing, but the stethoscope would come out and the thermometer would come out, and I was, 'Aw, c'mon let's see where it hurts.'"

Conrad, who was dutiful but uninspired during the infant stage, found that things changed "radically and progressively once they were talking and walking and more clued in to relationships." Now that his kids are growing up, he sees the long view of parenting: "It oscillates back and forth; it's not about equal parenting but a model where both parents are integrally committed to providing the structure for the kids, and where they can both navigate economic and professional possibilities that allow that to hold together."

Carter finds satisfaction in shared principles in action: "We believe in structure and consistency. Jessica knows the difference between being noisy outside and quieter inside. So it's not a question of always keeping her quiet or our being oblivious to the noise she makes. It's a question of appropriate situations. And she's very sensitive to that."

Paul, who had described a heart-wrenching alienation from his father ("I felt I was sort of a freak in his eyes," he told me) when he talked about what he expected from his own impending fatherhood, recounted a moment that signaled that the family curse had finally been broken. "The other night we were out there and I was sitting in the car and Beth was buckling Jacob in the baby seat in back, and my father goes, 'Good-bye, Jacob, I love you.' And I thought it was so nice. I thought I might feel jealous, but I wasn't. I was just so happy that he could express that.... It was dark, but I kind of felt like he was trying to say it to me, but it's so hard for him to do it.

"I was really close to *his* father, my paternal grandfather. But I think they had the same kind of relationship, where I don't think my grandfather was particularly warm to my father. But yet, being a grandfather, he gushed on me and he was really affectionate and quite close to me. And my father was a tyrant and never gave me much affection or praise. So it's nice to see that he was sort of becoming like my grandfather was to me, with Jacob—being warm and physical."

The moment took Paul back in time. "I remember with my father when I finally said to him—I was about twenty-seven—'Well, you always hated me,' and he goes, 'I don't hate you; I love you.' That was a turning point. Now he hugs me and kisses me, but he still can't say 'I love you.'"

Things will be very different for Paul's son. "I tell Jacob I love him a hundred times a day."

Nick can't recall the exact moment when he knew, just *knew,* that he was doing OK: "We didn't think we were good at it for the longest time. And then over time we realized that we were doing fine and our oldest was fine. She was tough, Emily. She used to throw fits and was extremely willful from the beginning. My initial way of dealing with that was to be just as willful and it was an endless battle. I don't know how that got resolved, but it did. And I guess when that resolved was when we realized we were all right; whatever happened, something went right, and that gives you confidence. It feels like a strong family."

So strong that perhaps there's more. "I've always thought that I'd have more time as the kids got older, and less rushing out and so forth, and I think that's possible. But now Martha is talking about adopting another kid, maybe being a foster parent, so who knows? I'm not totally reconciled to the idea, but I do think we're good at it—we have something to offer—and I miss having little ones. And when you think of raising another child, you know the ropes now, you know which baseball league is better, you know how to get a good soccer coach, or when to bitch about the teacher and all that stuff."

There is much uncharted territory to travel in search of shared parenting, much of it across the minefield of differences between men and women in general and individual men and women with their own expectations and histories. The map for sharing may turn out to look a lot like the map for parenting. As any parent will admit, one of the hardest parts of the job is to let those whom your every instinct is to protect make their own mistakes.

The same kind of willpower, when transposed into the adult relationship would translate into some counterintuitive moves for both mothers and fathers. For her, the supreme effort may be to step back and let dad make his own parenting mistakes and deal with the consequences. For him, it may mean taking the risk of finding out what kind of mistakes he would make; after all, coping with everyday failure is not part of the script most men have learned to read. Children, we are told over and over again, know when they are loved; there is no wrong way to love them—except, perhaps, not to go the extra mile of delivering the message.

CHAPTER EIGHT

CAN MEN HAVE IT ALL?

The Politics of Change

Every step away from a tangled situation, in which moves and counter-moves have been made over centuries, is a painful step, itself inevitably imperfect. Here is a vicious circle to which it is not possible to assign either a beginning or an end, in which men's over-estimation of women's rôles, or women's over-estimation of men's rôles, leads one sex or the other to arrogate, to neglect, or even to relinquish part of our so dearly won humanity. Those who would break the circle are themselves a product of it, express some of its defects in their every gesture, may be only strong enough to challenge it, not able actually to break it.

—Margaret Mead, *Male and Female*

THE EXPERIENCES THAT FATHERS HAVE NEGLECTED
and relinquished and are trying to reclaim are, not surprisingly, just those which have been glorified in motherhood: an

almost mystical nurturing instinct and a disposition to self-sacrifice, combined with an almost sacerdotal expertise in home management. Mother is, in effect, a veritable priestess to the mysteries of life. Not an easy role, on the one side, to take on; not an easy mystique, on the other, to give up.

Also not easy to give up are the perquisites that Father has gotten in return: the power to run the world, the freedom to come and go between public and private domains and to tailor the degree of involvement in family life to his temperament, taste, and interest at any time; in addition, Father has been granted the awesome power of economic, and sometimes literal, life and death over his dependents.

Ultimately, this dichotomy did all kinds of damage. Among other things, over time it deprived women of economic control over their lives ("Every woman with small children," Gloria Steinem used to say, "is one man away from welfare") and forced men to forfeit the keys to the emotional kingdom. Thirty years ago sociologist Jessie Bernard took note of the discrepancy between "His Marriage" and "Her Marriage," and zeroed in on the consequences: "As the pampered wife in an affluent household came often to be an economic parasite, so also the good provider was often, in a way, a kind of emotional parasite."

Crossing the terrain between those extremes toward a mutually enriching middle, where few have homesteaded, is what the women of the last twenty years and the men of the next twenty years are doing. It isn't easy and it won't be achieved in their lifetime.

As Mead points out, one generation can challenge the way things are, but they cannot transform the culture. That is frustrating but also inspiring. The efforts of contemporary fathers to combine work and love will not only make their lives richer; they also set the stage for real success in their children's generation.

The revolution is already well under way. And has been for the last twenty years. The advice feminist author Letty Cottin Pogrebin gave mothers in 1980 reflects a circumstance that has evolved beyond the unknown in the intervening decades: "What's tough is relinquishing your expert status and sharing domestic power before you are sure of gaining any external power to replace it." At the same time, Pogrebin's insight recognizes a reluctance to let go that is still with us. Fathers, too, need to make the unknown known for themselves—and to share some power. It is all of a piece, the entry of women into the workplace and the integration of men into the family.

EVERY DAY, IN EVERY WAY, IT GETS...

In day-to-day terms, the men and women trying to share their two worlds, to challenge old patterns, regularly run up against unexpected pockets of inexperience and ambivalence that intrude in every nook and cranny of both worlds. They also run up against the realities of how much of "all" one can really have.

Remember Mike? He is the devoted father who was jealous of his wife's ability to adapt her life to Delia, their new baby. Diane worked part-time and Mike tried mightily to have it all—the fast-track investment job, the travel, the pressure... and the Friday-morning play group at which he was the only father who showed up. He cuddled and consoled Delia, he fed her and changed her and now that she is two, he takes her out to dinner and reads to her in the evenings.

But all is not well. Last month Luke was born and now Diane is at her wit's end struggling with pressure to nurse Luke and to ensure that Delia doesn't feel neglected. She is exhausted, and Mike, who just got a major promotion, has gone on total overload. One night Diane lost it at the same time Luke did, and they were both on the bed wailing. Where was Mike? In the same room, resolutely reading his newspaper.

When confronted, all he could say was "I can't take any more. I can't take the baby stuff along with everything else." Everything else meaning the job, the marriage, the business trips, the financial responsibilities, *and* involved fatherhood with his first child. Mike has reached the crossroad. He can't have it all, and he is going to have to choose what part of the package he will let go of.

If he scales back on his work, even just the travel component, he will be off the partnership track in an instant. He will also be off the income rocket that enabled him to buy a large house for his growing family. If he scales back his involvement with his new son, he will miss the shared pleasures that bonded him with his daughter and will know the guilt of having shortchanged one child. If he promises himself that he will focus on Luke later, after the baby needs have been outgrown, he won't know Luke's moods and habits and interests when the time comes. If he keeps working and being unavailable to half his family, Diane's complaints will escalate. Her own conflicts about going back to work will be compounded by her perception that the baby is being neglected by one parent. And as she surveys her obligations, she will resent Mike's freedom to choose whether or not to be supportive. She can't believe that she has begun excusing Mike from responsibilities because he "brings home the bacon," a throwback to the fifties' cliché that Mike says he and Diane never thought would touch them.

Hard-driving men like Mike look at a limited array of scenarios. If he is really serious about equal parenting, he is going to have to leave the fast track to others—at least for the time being. Or if his job is the most exciting thing in his life, he is going to have to decide to go for it with a vengeance. And scale back on the rest. If he goes this route, he is going to have to renegotiate the terms of his family life to accommodate his revised priorities. He may or may not succeed.

In the same way that—finances apart, for the moment—some women are discovering that they feel most effective and fulfilled by staying at home full-time with small kids, some men are discovering that they, too, are drawn to full-time commitment to home (there is already a National At-Home Dads Association). By any measure of fairness or human potential, they are entitled to that choice. By the same token, some men (and women) will surely discover that they get more fulfillment from their work than from involvement with small children. They are entitled to that choice. Most are in between and see very few choices.

Mike is determined to find a third way, balancing both commitments. But, he concedes, "there is about a *thousand* pounds on either side of the balance. So I feel a great amount of pressure from all sides."

The work pressure is compounded by the way he shaves corners in order to squeeze in family life. "Every weekend I go home with fifty pounds of papers I am supposed to read. Most of the time I come back on Monday, and I haven't opened my briefcase. I don't do the preparation I meant to do. I come in Monday morning with a little trepidation. I pick myself up off the floor from doing puzzles with Delia, and I have to be Tom Wolfe's 'Master of the Universe' in the office. I ask myself if I am good enough to do this job. I'm a little intimidated."

But there is one element that is unusual in Mike's work life. "My boss has the same thing. He says he gets sweaty palms as he comes up the elevator on Monday morning." Mike, who is twenty-eight, and his boss, who is forty-five, find consolation and relief in the very unusual (for men) experience of sharing their frustration and conflicts over putting family first. The intimacy they have established transcends age and authority. Mike spent most of a long plane trip back from a business meeting "coaching" his boss "on how to make it work better for him. It's both about separation and integration."

Mike's advice reflects the unusual fluidity he brings to shifting gears from one side of his life to the other. It is a fluidity that most of the other fathers I spoke to couldn't even imagine, and this ability to make a series of transitions may portend some loosening up of the traditional home/office dichotomy among the younger men. "What I do at end of day," Mike told his boss, "is set a time when I want to be home. Say, I'm going to leave the office at 6:30, no matter what messages I have to return. I take them with me, return some in the car on the way home, play with kids, have dinner, and am on the phone again; I leave voice mail, call the coast.

I know I only have a window from six-thirty to eight-thirty with the kids. I push the business to either side of that time frame."

While the flow Mike is going with is hardly restful or organic, his boss is clearly locked into compartmentalizing the two sides of his life. "His approach," says Mike, "is not to leave the office until he has returned every message. He needs total closure—he needs to be able to say, 'I'm done with work, my desk is clean, I can go home.' That way he was staying at work till eight-thirty. By the time he gets home, the kids are asleep."

When he speaks of the need for "integration" between the two parts of his life, Mike strikes another chord that is more commonly associated with working mothers. Only his analysis has a distinctively male take: that it is the work that needs to be integrated into the family sphere. He advised his boss "'not to fight the fact that you are going to get interrupted at home with calls, faxes, conference calls.' In the summer I take every Friday off and I recognize that I'm probably going to have to be on the phone from nine to noon on Friday, but at least I'm there, and when I get off, I'm with the family. I try to not let it bother me. When I get on the phone and get engaged in a conversation, I am able to close out the world and be whatever role I need to be. I change the nature of my voice. I'm very serious. That's the way I do business. I'm direct, clear, and forceful when I'm doing business."

Sometimes the appearance of one persona in the script of the other is startling. "My wife says, 'Is that the guy I'm married to?'" Mike shares her dismay. "I like to be my personal self more than I like to be my professional self. Sometimes I carry my aggressive business style into my personal relationships as much as I endeavor not to do that." Summing up his efforts, he adds, "It is certainly the nature of my life that I am constantly shifting gears."

Even so, Mike doesn't have it all; he is missing some very important beats. First of all, he admits, he hasn't really found room for six-month-old Luke. His heart belongs to two-year-old Delia. "I love her so much I can't stand it. I rush home from work. Yesterday, I had a nine o'clock conference call, so I left work early so I could play with her, put her to sleep, and then got on my phone call. I'm spending more time with her than I ever have. I'm not spending time with Luke. I've got to get to that."

But the real toll is on his marriage. "I'm doing my best to make it work, but what doesn't get the fair amount of time and energy is my relationship with Diane. We are very fortunate that we have a strong bond and love each other very much, so that we can hold our relationship together, even if we're not putting the energy into it that it deserves. By the time I'm home and I've played with the kids, I'm so tired I can't see straight; unfortunately, that is the time that we've left to be together, and frankly neither of us has the energy to put into the relationship."

Unlike many men in his position, Mike knows he is not alone. "As I've gotten more senior and more comfortable with some of my colleagues, I don't need to put on a facade of being macho any more. We feel more free to talk about these things than I did when I was working my way up the ladder." As an example, he describes a Sunday-night conference call among several male executives to prepare for a big meeting with an important client. "The next day we all joked about how we all had our kids in the room while we were on this very important conference call, we were all nervous that our kids would interrupt. We learned that everyone's kids were making trouble. We were all trying to appear not distracted on this call."

Each of his colleagues would prefer, like Mike, "to have less on my plate." And each would probably echo his evaluation of where things stand. "I feel I'm doing a lot better than my father did in spending time with kids and trying to find balance in my life, but it is a real strain. I feel a lot of pressure to succeed as a father and at work."

The solution is clear to Mike. "I would love to do my job three days a week." The critical mass is building—witness those conference-call fathers—and the power is at hand.

"My boss and I have talked about doing a job share some-day." But the nature of the beast is considered immutable, as though its biology were destiny. "Our industry is so competitive. If we're only here three days a week and the other guys are on the job five or six days, can we have the continuity with clients to compete effectively? Currently we think not."

Most men regardless of their job have found that adaptability goes only one way. Because they find more support for parental policy than for parents, many are demonstrating more flexibility in their adaptations to the work world than they are getting back. For most, that adaptation means professional roads not taken.

The choice to limit work has clear financial and social consequences both in terms of prestige and access. It also has fallout in a quarter, the workplace community, that is a crucial source of support on most jobs; to coworkers, the message is unnerving and threatening. As Paul discovered to his dismay: "I had a collaborator, but that didn't work out. I think he got angry that I wasn't as interested in hanging out and going out for beers after work, but I really wanted to go home and be with my family."

Carl got a slightly different message from his closest co-worker. "We joke that he's more in love with his car than anything else. He can't fathom having children at this point. Nor can he understand the benefit of it. He feels that I'm nuts."

"Nuts" for giving up "success" as it is commonly understood. Many fathers who choose to put family first find that their anti-"success" choice makes them failures to some. The conventional measures of success lie in the public sphere—financial rewards, social status, and power over something or someone.

What may happen, though, as more and more men question this definition, is that the notion that work is the only route to achievement will be reconsidered, and the private sphere will be seen as the source of "pride and joy" for men that it has been for women. One-third of the men studied by Kathleen Gerson—the ones she labels "involved fathers"—told her that they were finding satisfaction in other components of their personal equation. The other two groups, the "autonomous men" and the "breadwinners," were much more dependent on their professional lives for their sense of accomplishment—or failure. One day soon maybe it will be possible for each individual to come up with a definition of success that reflects his or her own values.

THE NEXT GENERATION IS HERE

Carl and Paul and the "involved fathers" should be reassured to hear that reinforcements are on the way. Many of the young fathers I spoke to were generation Xers (born between 1965 and 1978) who are beginning to make their presence felt. They are already on record with the pollsters in support of balance. Many had begun preparing, with characteristic pragmatism, to build a life that would be conducive to family involvement even before they had built a family. That meant training in careers that would offer flexibility, marrying someone who feels the same, and choosing a place to live that would support their values. Judging by their aspirations, the culture-in-waiting values a mix of family, work, and social life—"The Triple Crown."

The polling firm of Yankelovich Partners, which has been monitoring lifestyle patterns since 1973, profiles these new adults in comparison to their predecessors, the baby boomers. They see work as a job rather than a career (63 percent vs. 40 percent for boomers) and don't expect to work in the same place more than five or six years. They see education as a way to "be financially well off" (75 percent in 1997) rather than to "develop a meaningful philosophy of life" (as 82 percent of the previous generation did). Almost 70 percent of both men and women agree that "having a child is an experience every woman should have" which is up from 45 percent in 1979. (Significantly, the same question was not asked about men.) The pollsters attribute the increased interest in childbearing to several factors, including the sense that boomer women gave up too much for their professional breakthroughs as well as the conviction that their generation will practice shared child rearing. The Xers also have a very pragmatic understanding of the trade-offs required. A recent MBA acknowledged that there are some roads that once not taken become impassible: "Our parents told us... 'You can do anything.' Yes, you can do anything. But you can't do *every*thing."

While such attitudes bode well for individual families, they are more ominous for overall social change. The pragmatism that recognizes human limitations is accompanied by a severe personal autonomy and a cynical view of the way the world works; 83 percent of Xers endorse the statement "People have to realize that they can only count on their own skills and abilities if they're going to win in this world." Instead of looking to the society at large for institutional support, they are focusing very intensely on an inner circle of friends— friends who look nothing like the "friends and neighbors" of olden days. Most of those friends are Internet relationships with shared "niche" interests and not a community in the sense of people who meet at school-board meetings and in the supermarket—and the voting booth. Participation in the electoral process, always lowest among the youngest voters, is particularly low in this group, leaving an enormous void in the arena where policy—and change—will be made.

As the younger men meet up with the older fathers who have been working in the dark to find private solutions to what are also public concerns, they are not joining forces to push for institutional change. That every-man-for-himself approach is worrisome. When they all emerge from their cocoons of exhaustion ten or twelve years hence, having launched their own children into the world, will that world be more compatible with the life experience they sacrificed so much for?

One such dad made his worldview very clear. When Martin asks himself what is better than when he was growing up he has a ready answer: "Ice cream. Beer. Computers. And, most of all, the fact that when I get all emotional—when I'm in a three-piece suit and my two-year-old comes into my office and I smooch him—no one says a thing. I have the ability to be a better parent." But when asked what he would do to roll the ball farther along, he replied that the only situation he could imagine that would galvanize him to take political action would be if his kids' school were being taken over by "religious fanatics." Barring that—so long as he has achieved balance in his own life—he is oblivious to the fact that without collective political action, his son's generation will be starting back at square one.

Yes, the understanding of fatherhood and its contribution to children's development is changing. Yes, the dynamic of marriage is changing. Yes, the nexus of time, money, and success is being broken apart. Yes, the priorities of a critical mass of people are changing. These changes pose hard questions about power, responsibility, leadership, family structure; about what money can buy; about how we value time;

about the state's responsibility to families and children. How are we going to address them? One by one? Or as a society?

Lawyer, scholar, and activist Mona Harrington has dealt with some of these questions in *Care and Equality: Inventing a New Family Politics.* She is clear and challenging on the vicious circle that we are in: "When families cannot provide the various kinds of care that their children or elders or others may need, and when public supports are not available because families are *supposed* to take care of themselves, the unmet need for care has to go somewhere. Generally it spills over onto public institutions that were not designed—and are not funded—to handle it." Schools. Courts. "Safety net" organizations. Hospitals. National policy changes are urgently needed if our society is going to take care of and bring justice to all. "The fact is—and it is an irreducible fact—the old formulas cannot yield both care and equality."

How will the pressures that are being addressed privately in homes around the country be brought into the public conversation? And how will the important public policy initiatives—on child care and early education, on universal health insurance not tied to a wage earner's job, on guaranteed family income, on a thirty-five-hour workweek and paid family leave, on family-friendly tax policy—become dinner-table conversation?

Instead there are regular reminders of how primitive the discourse still is. There was the Houston Oilers' offensive tackle, David Williams, whose pay was docked when he missed a game in order to be with his wife for the birth of their first child. Or Cleveland Indians player, Matt Williams, who missed a practice (!) for the same reason and was traded to the Arizona Diamondbacks in retribution. Or the case of a Maryland state trooper, Kevin Knussman, who was denied extended leave under the Family and Medical Leave Act to tend to his bedridden wife and newborn infant. He was told he was ineligible because "unless your wife is in a coma or dead, you can't be primary care provider."

The outrage that these incidents prompted is a measure of our readiness to examine what we want from our family and our work—and our heroes. And there are accumulating examples of how public support can change the rules. Four years after his leave was denied, Knussman was awarded $375,000 in the first-ever sex discrimination case brought under the Act, and in 1996, when his second child was born, he got a full twelve weeks of paid leave.

The momentum is picking up in Washington with such consciousness-raising prods as President Clinton's 1995 memorandum "requesting that all executive departments and agencies make a concerted effort to include fathers in their programs, policies, and research programs where appropriate and feasible."

Workplace changes made possible by the increasing acceptance of flextime and telecommuting are encouraging social scientists such as Ethel Klein to anticipate a performance standard based on the simple notion of "as long as the work gets done." As a society, she notes, "we privatize solutions until the pressure finally builds up and then we act." We are there now, Klein thinks.

But when I think of all the talking and marching and lobbying it took to bring about the first turn of the wheel—it took more than eight years to pass the Family and Medical Leave Act that Knussman sued under—I wonder where the muscle will come from for the second, the turn that mandates *paid* family leave, for example. Will the men who care so much about their children mobilize for all children?

POLITICAL PRESSURE

Family politics is where the equity frontier is. The vision of a world in which men are functioning members of a nurturing family is as much a feminist vision as is that of expanding opportunities for women. But while the first round of this two-part revolution was fought by women—largely because male resistance was the enemy—the next round must, by definition, include men. And women activists are wary of making a political alliance with men. They grew up on stories about men coopting the process, imposing power games and hierarchy on systems, and simply not "getting it."

Moreover, activists are preoccupied with maintaining the

two-steps-forward-one-step-back momentum of the feminist agenda; fighting for reproductive rights, welfare rights, the right to pursue one's sexual preference, and against international abuse of women, gender and racial discrimination, and economic inequities gives them plenty to do. When family issues emerge, they are the life-and-death issues of child abuse, deadbeat dads, battered women, and the impoverishment of single mothers. It almost seems a luxury to focus on the hassles of economically viable couples who are managing. Yet, as feminist strategists well know, those on the political right who *are* focusing political energy on "family values" have a very different idea of equity, marriage, and parenting. Ultimately, feminists understand that the family, where the dramas that shape the culture are played out, is an important frontier. As Gloria Steinem points out, "You will never have a true democracy without democratic families to nurture it."

DEEDS AS WELL AS WORDS

Another factor holding back the revolution may be the lack of conviction on the part of both men and women that men really mean it when they say they want to change the power structure. Mean it anywhere near as much as women did and do.

The experience of Sweden is often used to suggest the limitations of the fathering commitment. A *Harvard Business Review* article by Michael Kimmel summarizes the disappointing results of a decade-long effort to bring the men home: "The number of Swedish men who took formal parental leave rose to 44%; but again, fathers stayed home with their children for a much shorter time compared with mothers—an average of 43 days rather than 260." (And, remember, that leave is *paid*.) But the real imbalance shows up in the other half of the equation. According to Kimmel, "occupations are among the most sex-segregated in the world. Only 3% of executives are women. The wage gap is from 10 to 30%." As sociologist Linda Haas notes of Swedish policymakers, "There is no sign that they realize that the benefits to be gained by restructuring work in non-gendered ways might outweigh the personal costs to male stakeholders."

In other words, the Swedish experience is in many ways the reverse of that in the United States. They have made it possible for men to make their families a priority, but they have not made it anywhere near as comfortable for women to make career a meaningful part of their lives. It is entirely possible that it is the backwardness in the workplace that is keeping Swedish men from family life rather than their unwillingness to participate.

A more integrated experience has been achieved in neighboring Norway where, according to Charles Fishman writing in *Fast Company* magazine, "balance is the place where conversations about work and life begin."

Not only do Norwegians enjoy the familiar work schedule alternatives and paid leave options, but there is an appealing dedication to flexibility within the professional life cycle behind these programs, according to Fishman. There, he writes, "Diversity has to do with *perspective*—and it exists *within* individuals: Each of us is many different people at different times in our lives. Cultivate that diversity, and greater creativity will follow."

If American men *do* mean it, they are in a much better position than women ever were to promote institutional change. After all, as a group, men still have most of the power.

FINDING A THIRD WAY

Another reason that men need to be actively engaged in the process of reinventing the work/family system is that the Dreaded Tape and the Grinding Gears are part of the solution as well as part of the problem. Somehow we are going to have to mesh the two approaches. This is one battle that the General can't wage on her own.

The difficulty is that while women are steeped in expertise and insight about family life as they see it, most men can barely hear the tune, let alone set it to their own music.

As the men I interviewed described the pressures at play in their lives and tried to analyze what was going on, they were reasoned, respectful of all concerned, very polite—almost proper; they were almost totally lacking in the fire of outrage or the ice of irony that make for the self-deprecating humor that I've come to expect from women swimming upstream.

Comic actor Bill Murray made a similar observation and had an interesting explanation. "Women are actually funnier [than men] by nature," he told the *New York Times Magazine*. "They use a sense of humor in their life to make moments more bearable. Most men have no ability to laugh at themselves and that affects their sense of humor. They lose their rhythm."

The men in transition have "lost their rhythm" for the time being. How could it be otherwise when they are in the process of shifting gears and building new synapses, in effect, sounding out a new rhythm? In pursuit of an elusive goal they are making choices with consequences that are hard to anticipate: They cannot know the long-term cost of trading away income in the midst of a career or of putting a whole career on hold—usually their wives' but increasingly their own, too—for five or six years in expectation of creating a workable mix of time with children and income. Nor can they be prepared, any more than any parent ever could, for all the emotional and psychological risks a new kind of fatherhood may bring.

Their clumsiness can be very infuriating to their partners. The indulgence in the "I don't know nothin' 'bout birthin' babies, Miss Scarlett" defense. The retreat into forgetfulness, anger, or outer space. As a transition generation, they will continue to disappoint, more often than either would like, those they mean to impress.

The Grinding Gears are real, but they cannot be a cop-out. Men—men comparing notes with men—are going to have to figure out their own ways of doing their share of what needs to get done, and that means *knowing* what needs to get done. If women multitask better than men, men can't settle for doing one task in the time it takes a woman to do ten; they are going to have to learn how to do the same number of tasks in some equally efficient way of their own. By the same token, the Dreaded Tape, real as it is, needs to be disarmed as a weapon that oppresses the women who live with it and the men who live under it. My hope is that once men find their own ways of greasing the gears, we women will come to respect their ways—albeit maddening—of doing things, and perhaps even adopt a few for ourselves.

What would I say to the wives? What advice would I give myself? "Let it go," is the refrain that keeps circling. First of all, let go of the resentment that fuels the who-is-more-oppressed sweepstakes; let go of the need to control everything that pertains to home and kids; and, at the same time, let go of the sense of failure for what doesn't work, and wouldn't necessarily have worked anyway even if you had been in control; let go of some legalistic sense of what is "fair" and go for something that feels like teamwork; let go of a precise checklist of preconceptions of what a good father and husband is and wait and see how experience defines those roles in your relationship.

For the husbands, my advice is just the opposite. "Pick up," I say; not only your socks, but certainly your socks. Pick up on what is going on around you—the emotional landscape, the political climate, your own weather and its effect on others. Pick up the initiative—at home, at work, in the world. That will mean getting used to more failure and foolishness than you have been used to, but it is time to let go of that inflated sense of dignity that gets in the way of taking risks.

And most definitely pick up your power—the power that you have, even if you are not entitled to it, by virtue of being a man—and use it to turn around the very institutions that are bestowing it on you. Even a man who has traded away some of that power for experiences he values more could still call upon more influence than he does—in the service of those very values.

To both I would say, go for a marital partnership modeled on the good parent you are trying to be to your children. Start with an assumption of goodwill and commitment. Listen and really get to know the person you are dealing with. Be generous about their failings, encouraging about their successes, and willing to let them do things their own way.

How the Family Model Works—At Work

In the same way as a hierarchical division of labor is being overturned in the home, it will be dismantled in the workplace. It no longer makes sense for problems and solutions to travel up and down links of power, the absence of any one of which short-circuits the whole process. The circular image, of groups of people with complementary skills and familiarity with the whole process and a mutual commitment to goals is the one that makes room for family-responsive flexibility as well as for corporate nimbleness in the race to keep up with change. Moreover, study after study reminds employers that it will be the most desirable employees who will insist on jobs that reflect support for the extended context of a balanced life.

The most recent and unexpected development in Daniel's life suggests that we should pay more attention to the positive contribution the skills of family life can have in the "outside world." He is the physicist whose wife's career was booming while his was stagnant. Now, having so immersed himself in his daughter Ingrid's experience that he has become skilled at focusing on her and the details of family life, he finds he has become "hot" professionally. "In a way," he says, "it was easier when I wasn't in demand professionally. But, on the other hand, now that Ingrid is here, the choice, if I have to make it, is absolutely clear." In fact, the good father may be a better physicist. It is possible that his newfound ability to tune in to his surroundings and to focus on what is happening have made him a more desirable employee and a more astute scientist.

The adaptability that enables a mother or father to shift gears on a moment's notice when the unexpected strikes is also valuable in the employee who needs to respond to the challenges of the workday. The emotional characteristics that the good parent is cultivating in his or her own soul— empathy, teaching skills, cooperation, ingenuity, firmness, and commitment—are just the characteristics of "emotional intelligence" that Daniel Goleman sees in the "stars" of the successful workplace. These are the people who become leaders because they have built networks within the organization based on "communications, expertise, and trust." This kind of cooperative model is so effective, according to Goleman's research, because "highly adaptive, informal networks move diagonally and elliptically, skipping entire functions to get things done." Sounds like dinnertime in the average home—on a good day.

WHOSE REVOLUTION IS IT ANYWAY?

The men I interviewed want to liberate themselves as much as the women who came before them did and still do. But their process is different, so much so that women and even some like-minded men may not recognize it as revolutionary.

For one thing, while women in the seventies could focus their demands on individual men and "the patriarchy," men have no identifiable target for their frustrations. In the same way as there are few identifiable villains, there are even fewer identifiable heroes. Women could point to the first woman astronaut, the first woman Supreme Court Justice, the first female professional basketball player; however, there is no Hall of Fame for good dads. There is no pantheon of rebels performing dramatic photo ops, either. And it is hard to protest circumstances that are in many ways enviable. Changes that have already come about do make life good for a lot of fathers, even including those who want more of "it all." Most of them have a decent job with some family benefits and a wife who does her share of breadwinning. And they certainly spend more time with their kids than their own fathers ever did. So how can they complain, they worry, without sounding like they are whining?

Those men are right, I believe, to feel uncomfortable about joining up with any cause that could be called "men's lib." Organizations that have claimed or been saddled with that banner have for the most part seemed kooky, self-indulgent, or extreme. Politically they either have aligned themselves so closely to the women's movement that they operate like a gentlemen's auxiliary or have been so reactionary that their agenda would, in effect, undermine equality within the family. Unlike the soul-searching auxiliary groups, the family men I listened to describe a desire to focus on practical opportunities, although self-discovery will surely follow. Unlike the reactionary, return-to-traditions groups, their objective, as they see it, is not to get more control over their families but to get closer to the ones they love.

The tone changes, though, when their complaints are presented, not as the whines of individual men who want to have it all, but as a rallying cry to expand human options and make things better for families. Then, you have the potential for an agenda that is both personal and political. The agenda is "selfish" in the sense that it aims to achieve goals that enhance each father's self. It is revolutionary because it recognizes, as the feminist movement has done for over 100 years, that the problems today's fathers confront are, in fact, part of a larger political, social, and economic landscape that is tilted against the needs and realities of family life.

Looked at this way—as a movement to support families—the cause becomes more honorable and the battleground more familiar. Historically it has taken a higher cause—often literally protecting their families—to mobilize men. Today their families, all families, need protecting again, in this instance from the forces of a speeded up, hard-driving new world of work and from the outmoded expectations of what a man is supposed to be. Since the most oppressive of those expectations is that of the stoical, solitary warrior and since today's father wants to be emotionally engaged and collaborative, it may seem paradoxical to expect him to respond to a call to arms. But in many ways what a family movement must do is build new patterns within familiar frameworks. That involves breaking habits, challenging assumptions—and redefining terms. Despite its tender objectives, this campaign requires its own kind of assault on the way things are. A man who is determined not to let his children's lives pass him by has no choice other than to enlist, but the way he chooses to defend his priorities will redefine the notion of courage itself.

It takes courage to attempt a balancing act that often requires the impossible feat of being in two places at once. Failure, even against terrible odds, causes stress and guilt, and a discouraging sense of being misunderstood. For example, male colleagues may pat him on the back and mutter about wanting to be more connected to their own families, but nobody wants to hear that he is missing an important meeting to stay home with a sick kid. And if he does show up in the pediatrician's office, it is more likely that the other parents in the waiting room will be thinking, "He must be out of a job," rather than, "Oh, what a good father he is."

It takes courage to withstand that kind of negative feedback. Some of that courage comes from the moral support of sheer numbers, which is one reason men need to stand up and be counted, but numbers also build consensus, which is the groundwork of change. Every social movement is by definition political, and if votes begin to coalesce around family issues—tax relief, affordable child care, universal health insurance, a truly educational system—national policy will begin to change. But that isn't where the only drama is. "Policy," observes sociologist Rhona Rapoport, "is necessary but it isn't sufficient." Minds must change too. Example after example of individuals demonstrating a commitment to new priorities can be as persuasive as rank after rank of demonstrators with placards. Admitting that you can't take a promotion because you need and want to be with your children is a radical act, since it highlights a systemic situation that people have been handling as if it were a personal failure.

It takes courage to admit there is a problem. Men need to talk to each other the way women do in order to validate their experience—and laugh at the fixes they get into—and to keep sight of their objectives. Right now men often collude in the deception that a man's place is on the job—they leave their cars in a distant corner of the company parking lot so they can make a surreptitious getaway and they smile (warily, to be sure) at jokes about Mr. Mom.

It takes courage to see ridicule as punishment for breaking the rules. When women were beginning to expand the boundaries of the female role, the epithets were along the lines of Ms. Man. Women never wanted to switch roles (if anything, roles of all kinds are the problem); they simply wanted access to more kinds of experience—not all, but more. It was clear then, and it is even clearer now, that male human beings want and need more, too. They don't want to exchange roles, any more than women did. They simply want to expand their horizons to include family life.

It takes courage to explore new frontiers of child rearing. So far, parenting has been defined by how women do it. But as any woman can tell you, when men do it, they do it differently. This may be due to a lack of practice, a lack of will, or a biological imperative of their own—probably a combination of all those. The men I met are figuring out how to do what needs to be done in a way that utilizes their strengths and skills, a way that isn't their fathers' way either. One by one they are building a narrative of fresh insights into the parenting experience for all of us and offering their own children a richly expanded understanding of what life has to offer.

As more men become real parents, women and men are beginning to explore how the whole of family life can be shared. There, too, along with individual temperaments and histories, gender differences come into play. For a long time we thought that the differences between male and female roles were largely imposed by Western culture, and that as we achieved legal, economic, and political equality, those differences would disappear. Nowadays we have a more complex understanding of behavior. We know that certain responses are gender determined, while many other qualities, especially those having to do with nurturing and homemaking, seem much more culturally imposed than traditionalists would have us think.

In the face of so many variables each couple will have to devise their own form of teamwork. Every solution adds to the conversation, and the accumulation of those personal statements will change how we live. That is what revolution is about.

Above all, courage is the willingness to take risks. We tend to think of risk taking in terms of danger to life and limb. But the real risks are those that jeopardize the known in pursuit of the unknown.

The risks that men are taking in their relationships with their employers and their friends, as well as their wives and children, are daring in that sense.

That is why the men in this book are heroes, even though they would insist that all they want to be are "good dads." By reclaiming their place in everyday life and by finding their voice in the language of emotion, men like them will enlarge the possibilities for mixing and matching the ingredients of life for everyone. Not all men want to put family first, and— like the women who have chosen to build lives that do not include children—they should be supported in their choice. But the important thing for men and women is the choice, the opportunity to imagine one's self in a life composed of an array of roles that have not been predetermined.

The millions of individual dads who are discovering the pleasures of a dynamic relationship with their families are beginning to suspect that there are more men like themselves, although most are too busy putting one foot in front of the other to speak up. The increasing number of men who have begun to compare notes is building a powerful movement that will change the way we think of fatherhood, parenthood, and family—for the better.

What I hope fathers and mothers take away from this book is an understanding of how hard what they are doing is and how falling short is not a failure of will, but a result of the difficulty and the newness of the undertaking. They should know that their efforts are adding momentum to the transition from a society in which half of human experience has been off-limits to the other half of the population to one in which the rewards—and the joys—of work and family are available to everyone.

Bibliography and Books for Further Reading

Christopher Andersen. *Father: The Figure and the Force.* New York: Warner Books, 1983. Includes a poem on fatherhood by Erma Bombeck.

Michael P. Andronico, editor. *Men in Groups: Insights, Interventions, and Psychoeducational Work.* Washington, D.C.: American Psychological Association, 1996.

Eileen Appelbaum and Rosemary Batt. *The New American Workplace: Transforming Work Systems in the United States.* Ithaca, N.Y.: ILR Press, 1994.

Lotte Bailyn. *Breaking the Mold: Women, Men, and Time in the New Corporate World.* New York: Free Press, 1993.

Rosalind C. Barnett and Caryl Rivers. *She Works/He Works: How Two-Income Families are Happier, Healthier, and Better-Off.* San Francisco: HarperSanFrancisco, 1996.

Jessie Bernard. *The Future of Marriage.* New York: World Publishing Company, 1972.

T. Berry Brazelton. *Working and Caring.* Revised edition. Reading, Mass.: Addison-Wesley, 1992.

Adrienne Burgess. *Fatherhood Reclaimed: The Making of the Modern Father.* London: Vermilion, 1997.

Geoffrey Canada. *Reaching Up for Manhood: Transforming the Lives of Boys in America.* Boston: Beacon Press, 1998.

Ken R. Canfield. *The Heart of a Father: How Dads Can Shape the Destiny of America.* Chicago: Northfield Publishing, 1996.

Scott Coltrane. *Family Man: Fatherhood, Housework, and Gender Equity.* New York: Oxford University Press, 1996.

Bill Cosby. *Fatherhood.* New York: Berkley Books, 1987.

Carolyn P. and Philip A. Cowan. *When Partners Become Parents: The Big Life Change for Couples.* New York: BasicBooks, 1992.

Carolyn P. Cowan and Phyllis Bronstein, editors. *Fatherhood Today: Men's Changing Role in the Family.* New York: John Wiley & Sons, Inc., 1988.

Dorothy Dinnerstein. *The Mermaid and the Minotaur: Sexual Arrangements and Human Malaise.* New York: HarperCollins Publishers, Inc., 1977.

Barbara Ehrenreich. *The Hearts of Men: American Dreams and The Flight from Commitment.* Garden City, N.Y.: Anchor Press/Doubleday, 1983.

Susan Faludi. *Backlash: The Undeclared War against American Women.* New York: Crown, 1991.

Susan Faludi. *Stiffed: The Betrayal of the American Man.* New York: William Morrow & Company, 1999.

Ellen Galinsky. *Ask the Children: What America's Children Really Think about Working Parents.* New York: William Morrow, 1999.

Willard Gaylin. *The Male Ego.* New York: Viking, 1992.

Kathleen Gerson. *No Man's Land: Men's Changing Commitments to Family and Work.* New York: BasicBooks, 1993.

Carol Gilligan. *In a Different Voice: Psychological Theory and Women's Development.* Cambridge, Mass.: Harvard University Press, 1982.

John R. Gillis. *A World of Their Own Making: Myth, Ritual, and the Quest for Family Values.* Oxford and New York: Oxford University Press, 1997.

Daniel Goleman. *Emotional Intelligence: Why It Can Matter More Than IQ.* Reprint edition. New York: Bantam Books, 1997.

Ellen Goodman. *Value Judgments.* New York: Farrar Straus Giroux, 1993.

Edward T. Hall and Mildred R. Hall. *Hidden Differences: Doing Business with the Japanese.* Garden City, N.Y.: Anchor Press/Doubleday, 1987.

Mona Harrington. *Care and Equality: Inventing a New Family Politics.* New York: Alfred A. Knopf, 1999.

Sylvia Ann Hewlett and Cornel West. *The War against Parents: What We Can Do for America's Beleaguered*

Moms and Dads. Boston: Houghton Mifflin Company, 1998.

Arlie Russell Hochschild. *Time Bind: When Work Becomes Home and Home Becomes Work*. New York: Metropolitan Books, 1997.

Jane C. Hood, editor. *Men, Work, and Family*. Research on Men and Masculinities Series. Newbury Park: Sage Publications, 1993. Includes articles by Amy Andrews and Lotte Bailyn, "Segmentation and Synergy: Two Models of Linking Work and Family"; Joseph H. Pleck, "Are 'Family-Supportive' Employer Policies Relevant to Men?"; Polly A. Fassinger, "Meanings of Housework for Single Fathers and Mothers: Insights into Gender Inequality."

Jane Howard. *Margaret Mead: A Life*. New York: Simon & Schuster, 1984.

Mark Hunter. *The Passions of Men: Work and Love in the Age of Stress*. New York: Putnam, 1988.

Rosabeth Moss Kanter. *Men and Women of the Corporation*. New York: BasicBooks, 1977.

Michael Kimmel. *Manhood in America: A Cultural History*. New York: Free Press, 1996.

Michael S. Kimmel, Michael A. Messner, compilers. *Men's Lives*. 4th ed. Boston: Allyn & Bacon, 1998.

Elisabeth Kübler-Ross. *On Death and Dying*. New York: Macmillan, 1969.

Terry A. Kupers. *Revisioning Men's Lives: Gender, Intimacy, and Power*. New York: Guilford Press, 1993.

Michael E. Lamb, editor. *The Role of the Father in Child Development*. 3d edition. New York: John Wiley & Sons, 1997.

Ralph LaRossa. *The Modernization of Fatherhood: A Social and Political History*. Chicago: University of Chicago Press, 1997.

Ronald F. Levant with Gini Kopecky. *Masculinity Reconstructed: Changing the Rules of Manhood—at Work, in Relationships, and in Family Life*. New York: Dutton, 1995.

Harriet Lerner. *The Mother Dance: How Children Change Your Life*. New York: HarperCollins, 1998.

James A. Levine and Todd L. Pittinsky. *Working Fathers: New Strategies for Balancing Work and Family*. San Diego: Harcourt Brace & Company, 1998.

Steven Lewis. *The ABCs of Real Family Values: The Simple Things That Make Families Work*. New York: Plume, 1998.

Steven Lewis. *Zen and the Art of Fatherhood: Lessons from a Master Dad*. New York: Dutton, 1996.

Suzan Lewis and Jeremy Lewis, editors. *The Work-Family Challenge: Rethinking Employment*. London and Thousand Oaks, Calif.: Sage Publications, 1996.

Jeffrey Moussaieff Masson. *The Emperor's Embrace: Reflections on Animal Families and Fatherhood*. New York: Pocket Books, 1999.

Margaret Mead. *Male and Female: The Classic Study of the Sexes*. 1st Quill edition. New York: William Morrow, 1996.

Joan K. Peters. *When Mothers Work: Loving Our Children Without Sacrificing Our Selves*. Reading, Mass.: Addison-Wesley, 1997.

Joseph H. Pleck. *The Myth of Masculinity*. Cambridge, Mass.: MIT Press, 1981.

Letty Cottin Pogrebin. *Growing Up Free: Raising Your Child in the '80s*. New York: McGraw-Hill, 1980.

Kyle D. Pruett. *The Nurturing Father: Journey toward the Complete Man*. New York: Warner Books, 1987.

Stephan Rechtschaffen. *Time Shifting: Creating More Time to Enjoy Your Life*. New York: Doubleday, 1996.

Barbara Katz Rothman. *Recreating Motherhood: Ideology and Technology in a Patriarchal Society*. New York: Norton, 1989.

Juliet B. Schor. *The Overworked American: The Unexpected Decline of Leisure*. BasicBooks, 1991.

Pat Schroeder. *24 Years of House Work—And the Place Is Still a Mess: My Life in Politics*. Kansas City, Mo.: Andrews McMeel Publishing, 1998.

Pepper Schwartz. *Love Between Equals: How Peer Marriage*

Really Works. New York: Free Press, distributed by Simon & Schuster, Inc., 1995.

Jerrold Lee Shapiro. *The Measure of a Man: Becoming the Father You Wish Your Father Had Been*. 1st Perigee edition. New York: Berkley Publishing Group, 1995.

Shmuel Shulman and Inge Seiffge-Krenke. *Fathers and Adolescents: Developmental and Clinical Perspectives*. London: Routledge, 1997.

John Snarey. *How Fathers Care for the Next Generation: A Four-Decade Study*. Cambridge, Mass.: Harvard University Press, 1993.

Ron Taffel with Roberta Israeloff. *Why Parents Disagree: How Women and Men Parent Differently and How We Can Work Together*. New York: William Morrow, 1994.

Carol Tavris and Carole Wade. *The Longest War: Sex Differences in Perspective*. 2d edition. San Diego: Harcourt Brace Jovanovich, 1984.

Carol Tavris. *The Mismeasure of Woman*. New York: Simon & Schuster, 1992.

PUBLICATIONS AND ARTICLES

American Demographics magazine. P.O. Box 10580, Riverton, NJ, 08076-0580. Monthly publication charting consumer and lifestyle trends; pertinent articles include Diane

Crispell, "Chaotic Workplace," June 1996, and Cheryl Russell, "On the Baby-Boom Bandwagon," May 1991.

"Beyond Difference: A Biologist's Perspective." Anne Fausto-Sterling, adapted by Marty Mauzy. *Radcliffe Quarterly,* Cambridge, Mass., Radcliffe College Alumnae Association, Winter 1998.

Business Week magazine has published useful surveys of attitudes about work and family, edited by Keith Hammonds. 1221 Avenue of the Americas, New York, NY 10020-1095.

"Family Matters: A National Survey of Women and Men." The National Partnership for Women & Families. Lake Sosin Snell Perry & Associates, designer and administrator. Washington, D.C., February 1998.

"Fathers in America." The Gallup Organization. The Gallup Building, 47 Hulfish Street, Princeton, NJ 08542. 1996.

Mark Hunter. "The Last Time I Saw Daddy." *Men's Health,* July/August 1993.

Michael Kimmel. "What Do Men Want?" *Harvard Business Review,* November/December 1993.

Fortune, Betsy Morris. "Is Your Family Wrecking Your Career? (And Vice Versa)," March 17, 1997.

"The National Report on Work & Family: News on Legislation and Employer Policies." Business Publishers, Inc., 951 Pershing Drive, Silver Springs, MD 20910-4464.

"Relinking Life and Work: Toward a Better Future" A Report of the Ford Foundation based on a Collaborative

Research Project with Three Corporations (Xerox Corporation, Tanden Computers, Inc., Corning, Inc.) Rhona Rapoport, consultant-coordinator, 1996.

Sue Shellenbarger, weekly "Work & Family" columns in the *Wall Street Journal.* Since 1990, she has identified and explored a wide range of emerging topics.

Louise B. Silverstein, "Fathering Is a Feminist Issue." *Psychology of Women Quarterly*, v. 20, 1996.

The Washington Post/Kaiser Family Foundation/Harvard University Survey Project: Survey of Americans on Gender, March 1998. Kaiser Family Foundation, 2400 Sand Hill Road, Menlo Park, CA 94025.

VIDEOS

"Fatherhood USA" two cassettes: *Dedicated, Not Deadbeat* and *Juggling Family and Work.* Produced and directed by Marion Lipschitz and Rose Rosenblatt. Cine Qua Non, Inc. Executive producers James A. Levine and Ed Pitt, The Fatherhood Project at the Families and Work Institute.

ORGANIZATIONS

AFL-CIO (American Federation of Labor-Congress of Industrial Organizations), 815 Sixteenth Street, NW, Washington, D.C. 20006, (202-637-5000), *www.aflcio.org.*

Catalyst, an organization for professional women. Notable publications include: "Two Careers, One Marriage: Making It Work in the Workplace" and "National Report on Work & Family." 120 Wall Street, New York, NY 10005, (212-514-7600), *www.catalystwomen.org*.

Center for Women Policy Studies, 1211 Connecticut Avenue, NW, Suite 312, Washington, D.C. 20036, (202-872-1770), *www.centerwomenpolicy.org*.

Child Care Action Campaign, 330 Seventh Avenue, New York, NY 10001, (212-239-0138), *www.usakids.org/sites/ccac.html*.

Circadian Information (on shift work), 125 Cambridge Park Drive, Cambridge, MA 02140-2314, (800-878-0078), *www.shiftwork.com*.

Economic Policy Institute, 1660 L Street, NW, Suite 1200, Washington, D.C. 20036, (202-775-8810), *www.epinet.org*.

Families and Work Institute, a nonprofit organization addressing the shifting nature of work and family life. Publishes many studies, most notably *1997 National Study of the Changing Workforce* by James T. Bond, Ellen Galinsky, and Jennifer E. Swanberg, 1998; *Parental Leave and Productivity: Current Research,* edited by Dana E. Friedman, Ellen Galinsky, and Veronica Plowden, 1992; *Women: New Providers,* Whirlpool Foundation Study, conducted by Louis Harris and Associates, Inc., 1995.

330 Seventh Avenue, New York, NY 10001, (212-465-2044), *www.familiesandwork.org.*

The National Center for Fathering, P.O. Box 413888, Kansas City, MO 64141, (800-593-DADS), fax (913-384-4665), *www.fathers.com.*

National Center on Fathers and Families, University of Pennsylvania, 3700 Walnut Street, Box 58, Philadelphia, PA 19104-6216, (215-573-5500), *mailbox@ncoff.gse. upenn.edu*

National Fatherhood Initiative, 101 Lake Forest Boulevard, Suite 360, Gaithersburg, MD 20877, (301-948-0599), fax (301-948-4325), *www.fatherhood.org*

National Partnership for Women & Families (formerly The Women's Legal Defense Fund), published "Family Matters: A National Survey of Women and Men," February 1998. 1875 Connecticut Avenue NW, Suite 710, Washington, D.C. 20009, (202-986-2600), *www.nationalpartnership.org.*

New Moon Publishing, which publishes a bimonthly newsletter for parents of girls. P.O. Box 3620, Duluth, MN 55803, (218-728-5507), fax (218-728-0314), *newmoon @newmoon.org*

Radcliffe Public Policy Institute. 69 Brattle Street, Putnam House, Cambridge, MA 02138, (617-496-3478), *www. radcliffe.edu/pubpol.*

Women's Research & Education Institute. Published "Managing Work and Family: Nonstandard Work Arrangements Among Managers and Professionals," by Roberta M. Spalter-Roth et al., 1997, *www.wrei.org*

Yankelovitch Partners, Inc. "Monitor" studies of consumer lifestyles. 101 Merritt 7 Corporate Park, Norwalk, CT 06851, (203-846-0100).

INDEX

masculinity and, 37–38, 69–70,
179
need for openness among,
12–14, 23, 52, 69–74,
139–40, 215, 218–19,
238–39
perception of "having it all,"
8–9, 81–82, 209–41
sharing wage-earning status,
15–16
as single parents, 21
See also fathers and
fatherhood; Grinding Gears;
shared parenting
Men, Work, and Family (Hood),
159, 161, 162, 165
Men and Masculinity course
(Washington University),
37–38
men's lib, 235–36
Men's Lives (Kimmel and
Messner), 178
Mermaid and The Minotaur, The
(Dinnerstein), 25–26
Messner, Michael, 178
Meyers-Levy, Joan, 130–31
Microsoft, 131–32
Mommy's Rules, 9–12, 147
Mommy Track, 52, 74–75
mothers and motherhood
advice for, 230–31
breast-feeding and, 168,
172–74, 177–78
General role and, 126–28,
167–71
Mommy's Rules, 9–12, 147
Mommy Track, 52, 74–75

mother-only families, 36
mother's culture and, 22–23
reconsideration of, 9–12
and role models for fathers,
142–44
See also Dreaded Tape; shared
parenting; women
Murray, Bill, 177, 230

National At-Home Dads
Association, 214
National Fatherhood Initiative,
xix–xx
neglect, of children, 172
negotiation skills, 148–50
Nelson, Ozzie, 34
New Moon Network (magazine),
139–40
New York Times, The, 19–20, 56,
99–100
New York Times Magazine, The,
230
No Man's Land (Gerson),
156–57, 162–63, 220
Norway, 228–29
nursing. *See* breast-feeding

opting out, 113–16
Ozzie and Harriet (TV program),
34

parasitism, 210
parental leave, 18
argument for, 171